LIGHT AND LIFE

Grazyna Sikorska was born in Katowice in Polish Silesia.

In 1974 she was awarded an MSc degree at the University of Katowice, and came to England to continue her scientific research. For a time she worked with the Polish Catholic émigré weekly *Gazeta Niedzielna*, and in 1979 joined the staff of Keston College, the centre for the study of religion in communist lands, researching all aspects of religious life in her native country.

Grazyna is married to Janusz, whose Polish parents found themselves in England after the war. They met at the Polish Catholic Chaplaincy in London, of which Janusz is Chairman. They have two children, Sławomir and Katarzyna. and live in Kent.

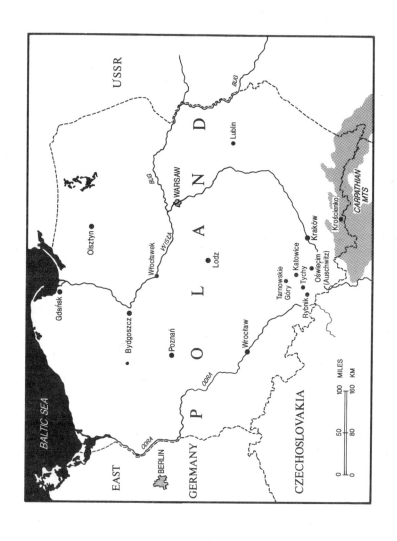

LIGHT AND LIFE

*

Renewal in Poland

GRAZYNA SIKORSKA

With a message from
POPE JOHN PAUL II

William B. Eerdmans Publishing Company
Grand Rapids, Michigan

First published 1989 in Great Britain by
Fount Paperbacks, London.
This edition published 1989 through special arrangement with
Collins Publishers, London, by
Wm. B. Eerdmans Publishing Co., 255 Jefferson Ave. SE,
Grand Rapids, Michigan 49503

Library of Congress Cataloging-in-Publication Data

Sikorska, Grazyna.
Light and life.

"First published 1989 in Great Britain by Fount Paperbacks,
London"—T.p. verso.
1. Blachnicki, Franciszek, 1921–   .   2. Catholic
Church—Poland—Clergy—Biography.   3. Church renewal—Catholic
Church—History—20th century.
4. Poland—Religious life and customs.   I. Title.
BX4705.B527S55   1989   282′.092 [B]   89-11650
ISBN 0-8028-0341-5

TO MY CHILDREN

CONTENTS

ACKNOWLEDGEMENTS

I would like to thank the many friends and colleagues of Father Franciszek Blachnicki, both in Poland and in Carlsberg, and in particular Maria Skop (Gizela), his personal assistant; the members of Light-Life who shared with me their Oasis experiences; Marite Sapiets for her critical observations on my manuscript; Father Tadeusz Kukla for always being available when I needed him; and my husband Janusz for his constant support.

I met Father Blachnicki through an act of God's providence – the many hours I spent talking with him will forever be an inspiration to me. I want to thank God for this. I hope that in a small way this book will help towards repaying my indebtedness to Father Franciszek for rejuvenating my faith.

FOREWORD

On 27 February 1987 Father Franciszek Blachnicki, the founder of the Polish renewal movement "Light-Life", died in exile in the small West German town of Carlsberg. At his funeral a message was read out from his friend and protector Pope John Paul II:

> God has taken Father Franciszek Blachnicki and his death has filled many hearts with sorrow. We have lost a devoted apostle of conversion and spiritual renewal as well as a great spiritual leader of young people. It was because of his inspiration that a specific form of "Oasis Life" was born in the Polish Land. He used the talents abundantly bestowed upon him, his intellect and heart, and the unique charisma given to him by God, to build God's Kingdom. He built it with prayer, work and suffering. He built it with such determination that we rightly think of him as "God's fool". We thank God for all the good he aroused in people. We pray fervently that his soul enjoys fullness of light and life. From my heart I bless those who will continue his work, his colleagues, family, friends and all those participating in the funeral.

John Paul II

Though relatively unknown in the West, Father Blachnicki had been one of the leading figures in Poland's troubled history since the Second World War. While for many he was Poland's "Gandhi", the communist authorities described him as "a Polish Ayatollah" and "a theologian of hatred and national treason". Special meetings were held by the Central Committee of the Polish Communist Party in which ideologists sought to discredit him and smash the Light-Life movement. If the communist authorities fear Light-Life, it is not only because as many as half of the young priests in Poland have come from within its ranks, nor even because half a million Poles have participated in the movement's summer "Oasis" camps. What they fear most is the uncompromising and dynamic Christianity displayed by the movement's members and their determination to reshape Communist Poland into a truly Christian society.

1

In Search of Christ

The year 1918 marked not only the end of the First World War but also the collapse of the established order in Central and Eastern Europe. Nine new states were created in the void left by the disintegration of the defeated powers, Germany, the Austro-Hungarian Empire and Tsarist Russia. Among these nine the Polish Republic was re-formed after over 120 years of political nonexistence. It faced the almost impossible task of reuniting into one entity the three parts of Poland which since 1795 had been incorporated into three partitioning states – Austria, Prussia and Russia. However, before any reintegration could begin, the difficult problem of frontiers had to be solved. Among many controversies generated in the process of delineating Poland's borders was the complex problem of Silesia in the South West. The importance of coal, in which the area was very rich, made it a land stubbornly sought after by both Germany and the new Polish state. Except for its western areas the population was ethnically mixed.

The towns were almost entirely German yet most of the agricultural districts were Polish. In the end it was decided at the Treaty of Versailles to carry out a plebiscite among the local inhabitants.

On 20 March 1921 over one million Silesians went to the polls to decide the future of the region. In the small town of Rybnik, Maria and Józef Blachnicki went to cast their votes. Józef – whose grandfather had participated in the unsuccessful uprising of 1861 against the Russians and had settled in Silesia to avoid being deported to Siberia – probably voted for Poland. For Maria (née Müller) the situation was far more complex. Her grandparents had come to Silesia from Wittenberg and could hardly speak Polish. Yet Maria's own mother felt so much of a Pole that she refused to speak German at all. Maria was pregnant, just a few days from her confinement. What future did she want for her baby and her other four children? Whatever the individual choices made by Maria and Józef, 65.2% of Rybnik's inhabitants chose Poland. Four days later, on 24 March 1921, the Blachnicki's fifth child, Franciszek, was born in a Polish Rybnik.

At this time Józef was working as a senior male nurse in a local private hospital. It was not a lucrative job. Yet he earned enough to support his large family. After leaving Rybnik the family lived for a few years in the small Silesian town of Orzesze before finally settling down in Tarnowskie Góry – the main town of a small administrative district. By then the Blachnickis' last child Henryk had been born. Maria was now forty-three years old and was suffering from a severe kidney disease – the illness forced her to delegate many of the household burdens and duties to her two daughters, fifteen-year-old Ada and Ela, who was a year younger. Despite Maria's illness the Blachnickis had a very happy home. Neither parent was strict. Instead, a form of self-discipline was imposed by Ada and Ela, who were increasingly involved in bringing up their three younger brothers, Ernest, Franciszek and Henryk. It was the two sisters rather than the parents who had the greater formative influence on the three boys. Ela taught them discipline and a practical approach to life; Ada contributed artistic sensitivity. Franciszek and Henryk also owed their education to their sisters.

These were the mid-1930s and the world economic recession had not passed Poland by. Józef's employers closed down several hospitals – including the one in Tarnowskie Góry. He was forced to take an early retirement and in consequence the family had to leave their comfortable quarters on the hospital premises and find more modest accommodation in the town. Even more important however, the education of the children was in jeopardy. There was not enough money to pay the school fees for everyone. One evening Ada and Ela summoned a family meeting and informed their parents that they had decided to give up grammar school, instead they would take up clerical work. The additional income would go towards paying fees for the two academically-inclined boys – Franciszek and Henryk. At first the parents were taken aback by their resolute daughters but in the end they agreed.

Maria and Józef were not very religious. They hardly ever went to church, nor did they make their children attend Sunday Mass. However, they saw religion as an integral part of the Polish cultural tradition which should be preserved. Józef sang in a church choir but mainly to satisfy his passion for music. The whole family often participated in an annual pilgrimage to the nearby Marian shrine of Piekary, not primarily out of spiritual need but because they considered it a pleasant family outing. Even their celebration of Easter and Christmas, however grand, was not as elaborate as that of Maria's birthday – the most important event for which the entire family gathered together.

For Franciszek, religion acquired a new importance when he went to school. Like all other boys he had to attend religious education lessons, compulsory in Polish prewar schools, as well as school Masses. He always had the best marks in religion and after he wrote a particularly moving essay the catechist held him up as a model Catholic boy – Franciszek was embarrassed! He had the highest marks not only in religious education but in all other subjects, without any real effort on his part. Since early childhood Franciszek had been searching for a clear, integral vision of life and a way to shape a better world. Religion, which he saw as a mere compilation of never-ending duties, rites and prohibitions, seemed to him totally irrelevant. It was the Scout movement and its activities, designed to develop an individual's abilities and then to harness this individuality for the good of the community, that appealed to Franciszek.

He had become a Scout at the age of ten following Ela's example. From the start he liked the methods adopted by the Scout movement. Its encouragement of active self-expression and the desire to learn, its closeness to nature, and its system of patrols in which boys of the same age educate each other, with an older one always at hand ready to help – principles which form a bond of brotherhood among Boy Scouts throughout the world. He admired abstinence from alcohol, a specific feature of Polish Scouting. Franciszek's eldest brother Rudolf, thirteen years his senior, was a heavy drinker. Drunken brawls witnessed by the younger children made Franciszek a staunch anti-alcohol campaigner. Although in his final year at school only half the class were Scouts, at Franciszek's insistence there was no alcohol at the graduation ball. In time his attitude to religion changed as he accepted Baden-Powell's ideas of humanism backed by religion, regardless of creed. Slowly he began to appreciate the educational role of religion.

Franciszek rose rapidly in the Scouting movement. As a teenager he was already a Scoutmaster for the district of Tarnowskie Góry. "I went to school only in my free time", he once said laughingly, "my main occupation was Scouting." Even when he was sitting his final exams at the grammar school, he managed to lead a camp between the written and oral exams. Scouting had become for him a kind of ideology. He sincerely believed that the whole world could be reshaped in accordance with the movement's humanitarian principles. Doing good would become the aim of life for every citizen of our planet. This model of the perfect future world had just one defect. Franciszek knew that in real life "Right" was so often defeated by "Wrong", which seemed more powerful. Then one day he "found" a golden formula, "power should be secured in the hands of good people". Only much later did he understand that good imposed by force ceases to be good.

It was spring 1938 and Franciszek, just seventeen, was sitting his final exams. It was obvious that he would go to University but nobody, not even himself, was sure what subject he should read. He liked and was good at so many. One thing Franciszek was absolutely sure of – he would not study theology. In the end he settled for political economy and dreamt of a diplomatic career or some kind of work for the public good. However just then a new law made it compulsory for all secondary-school leavers to spend a year in army service at a military college before they could enter university. Franciszek left his military college in June 1939 and went for two months of military exercises to an infantry regiment in Tarnowskie Góry. He was due to return home on the first of September.

On 31 August at 8 p.m. Sturmbanfuehrer Alfred Naujock of the Nazi Security Service led an attack on the German-language radio station at the German Silesian town of Gleiwitz. His men included a dozen convicted criminals, referred to in his orders by the codeword "Konserwen" (tin cans), who had been promised a reprieve in return for their cooperation in a provocative "Polish" action against the local Germans. After a brief encounter with the station guards, they burst into one of the studios, broadcast a "patriotic announcement" in Polish, sang a rousing chorus, fired a few pistol shots and left. Once outside, the "tin cans" were mown down by the machine guns of the SS. Their bodies, carefully dressed in blood-soaked Polish uniforms were abandoned where they fell, to be found in due course by the local police. Before the night was out, the world was awakening to the astonishing news that the Polish Army had launched an unprovoked attack on the Third Reich. At 4.40 a.m. on 1 September the German battleship Schleswig-Holstein opened fire on the Polish port of Westerplatte on the Baltic coast. One hour later the Wehrmacht tore down the barriers at the border points, including those at Bytom just ten miles from Tarnowskie Góry. Franciszek's regiment was stationed in the nearby forest. That night Franciszek was on sentry duty, already thinking about University, his future. Suddenly he heard the sound of machine guns coming from the south-west. The Second World War had begun.

By 6 September, the Polish command had abandoned its plans to defend the frontiers. By the end of the second week Poland's capital Warsaw was surrounded. Then, on the 17 September, uninvited and unannounced, the Soviet army crossed the eastern frontier. The Polish forces were now caught in a trap with no wall against which they could lean their backs and fight. The Polish President and the Commander in Chief both crossed into Romania, only to be interned. One by one Polish units capitulated and the last Polish unit surrendered at Kock on 5 October. After that, the Poles could only fight abroad or in the underground movement.

The division of spoils was arranged by a German-Soviet pact signed on 28 September. A demarcation line was fixed along the rivers Bug and San, to which the Wehrmacht now withdrew. For practical purposes this line was regarded as a permanent frontier. Both zones of occupation were subjected to unrestrained political engineering by their respective conquerors. On the German side of the demarcation line, the territory was divided into two parts. The northern and western areas, including the whole of Polish Silesia, were directly annexed to the Reich. The rest was formed into a separate so-called "General Government". In neither case, whether inside the Reich or outside it, did the population enjoy the protection of civil law. All the occupied territories were designated as law-less Arbeitsbereich (work areas). Martial law was in force and death or the concentration camp were the only two forms of stipulated punishment for any type of offence. To all intents and purposes, the whole of the German zone of occupation became "Gestapoland".

When Franciszek's unit capitulated at Tomaszów Mazowiecki at the end of September, he became a prisoner of war. However on his way to a camp he managed to escape and using the skills learnt in his Scouting days found his way back to Tarnowskie Góry. Almost immediately he joined the flourishing resistance movement. In the early months of the war scores of partisan groups took to the woods; hundreds of conspiratorial cells were formed spontaneously everywhere, including Silesia. At the beginning, Franciszek's involvement in the resistance movement was rather amateurish and based solely on his old Scouting contacts. With a few friends he stole a local Scout troop banner from a German warehouse. They also transcribed and disseminated BBC programmes. In time a more conspiratorial system of "threes" was introduced: no more than three persons knew of each other in order to limit the scale of arrests in case of Gestapo infiltration. By the spring of 1940 a Polish Partisan Organisation had been founded in Tarnowskie Góry, which was later to become part of the Home Army, the AK (Armia Krajowa). Nineteen-year-old Franciszek was appointed its leader in the town.

Most people, including Franciszek, were impatiently waiting for Hitler's attack on France, convinced that this would inevitably bring German defeat and the end of the war. Meanwhile the resistance movement was growing in strength and numbers. One afternoon in March 1940 Franciszek was holding a recruitment meeting with a party of former non-commissioned officers. At the end of the meeting Franciszek warned all those present against a certain Mr Bieniek, a Gestapo informer, who was posing as a patriotic Pole and trying to find a way into the Resistance. No sooner had he finished than a man stood up and announced loudly: "I am Bieniek." There was visible consternation among all present. To defuse the situation Franciszek pretended that he believed Bieniek when he tried to persuade everyone that he was indeed a loyal Pole. A few days later he knew that Bieniek had reported the meeting to the Gestapo. There was no time to lose. Franciszek had to escape and all those present at the fatal meeting had to be isolated from any further contact with the Resistance. He was ordered to go to Zawichost, a little town in the eastern part of the "General Government". There, a technical college which took boarders was still operating freely. Franciszek became an assistant to the school gardener while waiting for his false identity card. With it he was planning to escape to France via Hungary and join the Polish army being formed there. He was however ordered to stay in Zawichost. The German attack on France seemed imminent as did their expected defeat. Franciszek was waiting for the end of the war.

On Sunday morning, 27 April 1940, the Gestapo cordoned off the school. After a preliminary search the Germans ordered that all pupils and staff should gather in the school yard. Franciszek never expected that the raid had anything to do with him. He thought that the Germans simply wanted to check everyone's association with the school, and went outside without hesitation. In front of the school yard steps stood a small group of Gestapo officers. Among them Franciszek suddenly recognised two from Tarnowskie Góry. He had however no choice but to walk straight towards them. An officer asked Franciszek whether he came to Zawichost from Silesia; the first alarm bells began to ring. He still had his old identity card and therefore had to tell the truth. He was asked his age, then whether he was an officer cadet in the Polish Army and at last, "Is your name Blachnicki?" He knew by then it was not just a routine Gestapo raid; they were out to capture him. When Franciszek nodded his head one of the officers, Hartman (who was later in charge of the investigation), sprang up and hit him so hard that Franciszek fell to the ground. "Do you know what is in store for you?" he asked Franciszek while he was struggling to stand up. "Yes" answered Franciszek and pointing to his neck enacted an execution. Surprisingly Hartman apparently showed some human feelings at this moment and re-assured Franciszek, "Maybe it won't be so bad."

Franciszek knew his situation was critical. On lea-ving Tarnowskie Góry he had advised his colleagues to blame him in the event of them being caught by the Gestapo; he should have been safely in France by now out of the Gestapo's reach. Indeed many had given Franciszek's name as the one who had recruited them to the Resistance. The Gestapo were convinced Franciszek was an important catch. During the two weeks prior to the start of his interrogation Franciszek racked his brains as to how he should give evidence. Would he be able to withstand the pain of possible tortures? In the end he chose his course. He was not going to deny any fact already known to the Gestapo as this would only enrage them. Instead he carefully composed a detailed and logical story, filling all existing gaps with fantasy. Using secret messages and during daily walks he shared his story with his imprisoned friends in order to avoid any contradiction between statements. Franciszek decided to tell the Germans that he was only the leader of the military section and that the meeting attended by Bieniek was the first that he had organised. The only difficult problem was the name of the person who had recruited Franciszek into the Resistance. He chose to give a fictitious name and description and say that the arrangements had been made by letter. The interrogation was going very smoothly. Hartman was so pleased with Franciszek that he let him go home on a visit, during which he saw his mother for the last time.

When however forty pages of the official record were ready for signature, Hartman turned to Franciszek and said, "I see through your tactics. You have told us only what we already know. You have not given me any new names!" But he could not prove anything and so following Gestapo practice Franciszek was interned in Auschwitz concentration camp indefinitely. When his sister Ada went to make enquiries to the Gestapo about Franciszek, she was told that he had been sent to a special "correction camp". Once a month an almost identical letter arrived from Auschwitz assuring the family that he was healthy and that conditions at the camp were good. Only several months later did the horrifying truth about Auschwitz begin to filter through.

Franciszek arrived at the camp in one of the very first transports. In the yard of what until recently had been an army camp, prisoners were doing endless press-ups and other exercises under Gestapo supervision. The camp was still in the process of organisation, former army buildings were being transformed into camp barracks and the system of blocks was being worked out. All prisoners were given striped clothing and were tattooed with a number. Franciszek became number 1201. One day he was summoned to camp headquarters and without any explanation was ordered to sew a black spot onto his trousers and jacket underneath his camp number. He was the first prisoner to be given such a spot and had no idea what it meant – he was soon to find out. Returning to his barracks every passing SS man slapped his face. Franciszek now knew that the black spot was to single out prisoners who were destined for "special treatment". A few of his friends were given the same black spot, as were all the Jews and priests in the infamous "punishment block thirteen". The Kapo who was chosen to organise block thirteen was a notorious criminal and sadist. His ultimate daily aim was to be able to report at the evening roll-call, "ohne Juden" (without Jews).

The first task allocated to those in the punishment block was to pull the notorious Auschwitz roller. Long shafts were attached to its ends and sixty prisoners – the entire block - had to run pulling the roller in the camp yard for eight hours every day, with a short break for lunch. SS men kept the running pace going using whips. Many were killed at the roller even though the younger men took the outside places so that the lashes fell on them. The food rations in Auschwitz allowed a healthy person to survive for about three months. Outside the punishment block there was some chance to organise extra food. For the inmates of block thirteen, isolated from the camp behind a high wall, there was no such possibility. Not surprisingly ten people died on average each day, so that the entire punishment block, which had grown to three hundred men, could have been dead within a month.

One day the Auschwitz commandant, Frycz, came to block thirteen and announced an amnesty for all who had spent more than four months there. Four prisoners walked out, including Franciszek. It was November 1940. Franciszek learned that many colleagues from his Silesian transport, who had so far survived, had become a kind of aristocracy in the camp as they could speak very good German. Thanks to them Franciszek became an SS Einkaufer (buyer). He had to do the shopping for the families of the SS guards living near the camp. It was an easy job – just two hours a day. He now lived in a special barracks for some 100 prisoners who had contact with SS men. It was clean and the food was much better. However, this good spell was not to last for long. In one SS man's house there lived a Polish servant girl. She somehow managed to obtain badly needed medicines which Franciszek smuggled into the camp. One day she gave him a box of medicines wrapped in a piece of paper and tied with an elastic band. Franciszek quickly threw it into an empty milk container while he took some food to an SS house 400 yards from the path. He left the container on the path without giving even a second thought to it. When he returned he saw to his horror that the packet was lying next to the container. Franciszek quickly thought the matter over.

If a passing SS man had found it he would certainly have taken the packet with him, so Franciszek decided

to take the packet back into the camp. Safe in his barracks he read a letter from the Polish servant girl. In it
she asked Franciszek to gather information about life
in the camp and to pass it on through her to a local
Resistance group. While he was reading the letter he
heard an announcement through the camp loudspeakers
summoning him to camp headquarters. Automatically
he put the letter in his pocket and left quickly. He was
not worried, certain that as so often before it meant that
there was some additional shopping to be done. However, when he arrived at the headquarters, the camp
commandant himself, accompanied by his deputy and
the officer in charge of his block, was waiting for him.
The commandant threw himself at Franciszek shouting
"Where is the Polish letter? This is the end." Franciszek
knew that people had lost their lives for smaller offences
than contact with the Resistance and expected to be
executed on the spot. Instead he was taken to the bunker,
a camp prison situated within the punishment block.

A few days later the interrogation started. Franciszek
maintained that he was innocent. He had intended to
hand the letter in after he had read it. The Germans
did not believe him. They beat him up again and again
but Franciszek would not change his story. Franciszek
was confronted by Hartman, who had travelled from
Tarnowskie Góry to Auschwitz to inform Franciszek
in person that he was to face a trial. The Gestapo
had arrested several other members of the Resistance
and during their interrogation it had been established
beyond all doubt that Franciszek was the Resistance
chief for the town. A few days later, Frycz inspected the
bunker, talking to all the prisoners. He asked Franciszek
why he was there. When he learnt of Franciszek's

Silesian origin he burst into a hysterical shout, "You swine. We liberated you from Polish enslavement and you repay us with such ingratitude. You had better find a piece of rope and hang yourself, for you will not leave the bunker alive." And with this he left the cell.

Hardly fifteen minutes had gone by when the officer in charge of the block came and ordered him out. Franciszek thought he was going to be shot but the officer led him to punishment block thirteen. There Franciszek survived another four months and was reprieved again. Even Franciszek found it difficult to believe his "luck". To survive two spells of four months in the punishment block and a month in the bunker was close to being a miracle. Certainly it was the only case of this type in the horrific history of Auschwitz.

Soon after, Franciszek was handed an official indictment by a prosecutor. He was charged with high treason – an attempt to annex a part of German territory by force. For such a crime the German penal code prescribed the maximum penalty – death. Before Franciszek was allowed to leave the camp he had to undergo a period of quarantine. It was during this time that he heard of the death in the bunker of Maximilian Kolbe, a Roman Catholic priest who gave up his life for a fellow prisoner. The news disturbed him, but he could not grasp the motive behind the priest's decision. Finally after signing a pledge that he would not disclose anything that he had seen in Auschwitz, Franciszek was ready to leave the camp. He was taken to a prison in the town of Katowice and on 30 March 1941 he was put on trial together with two close friends from the Resistance. At the end of the one-day trial, sentence was passed. Franciszek and Władysław Kurek, who was the Resistance leader for the whole district of Tarnowskie Góry, were condemned to death; the third prisoner was sentenced to twelve years of strict regime concentration camp. Władysław and Franciszek were handcuffed and taken to B1 – the condemned section of the prison in Katowice. In the corridor outside the courtroom Franciszek noticed his father and his sister Ela. He could not talk but pointed only with his hand to his neck. Ela fainted. His father tried to cheer him up and promised to move heaven and earth to get him reprieved.

The first thing which struck Franciszek on entering B1 was the silence – the kind of silence experienced when visiting a ward of terminally-ill patients. He could almost touch the death in the air. Like all the other condemned men he was handcuffed; the handcuffs were removed only for short periods during meal times. There were three prisoners in each cell. Franciszek became acquainted with his two fellow inmates. When he went for his first walk in the prison yard, the sad slowness of the walk reminded Franciszek of a funeral march. He found consolation in the thought that whatever happened he still had four weeks of life before him – that was how long the appeal procedure would last. The chance of a reprieve was slim indeed but everyone clung to a thread of hope. If after four weeks, execution was not carried out, it meant that the case had been referred to a higher office in Wroclaw and gave a condemned prisoner another six weeks to two months of life. Occasionally a case was referred to Berlin, to the Minister of Justice or to the Führer himself, and then it could be another few months before a final decision. There was also a traditional law in Germany, respected even during the war, that unless the death sentence was carried out within ninety-nine days of his condemnation, the prisoner was automatically reprieved. Like everyone else, Franciszek wrote a long appeal against the sentence and buried himself in books. There was a good prison library with both Polish and German books. Life would have been almost bearable if it had only been possible to forget, not to think constantly of the future. However, a few days after his arrival at B1, Franciszek was brutally reminded of the gravity of his situation. It was the evening of Good Friday. Everybody was already in bed. Suddenly there were whispers, steps in the corridor. Then the door to his cell was opened. There stood the governor of the prison with a few other people behind him. A young boy, who had been helped by Franciszek to write a letter to his parents earlier that day, was summoned. He got up from his bed and calmly left the cell. The doors of other cells were opened one by one and a few other names called out. Then the tense silence prevailed once again. It all happened so swiftly that Franciszek kept looking at the empty bed almost having to persuade himself that the unthinkable did happen – people were being taken out to be executed.

It was Franciszek's ninetieth day in B1. The executioner was coming that day from Wrocław. He used to come once every two weeks. Franciszek was convinced that he was going to be beheaded that night – beheading was the method used by the Germans at that time. That afternoon he wrote a farewell letter to his family and sat on his bed waiting. A few hours later the guards walked slowly down the corridor. The adjacent cell was that of Władysław Kurek. The guards stopped outside it. They opened the door. "Władysław Kurek", they called him out. "This is the end," thought Franciszek. The guard stopped in front of his cell and put the key into the lock. Franciszek stood up and started to walk slowly toward the door – to cut short the intolerable waiting. The guard hesitated, turned the key in the opposite direction, pulled it out and went to the next cell; he had made a mistake by one number. Franciszek knew he was going to be reprieved.

On 14 August - exactly on the first anniversary of Maximilian Kolbe's death in Auschwitz, Franciszek was officially informed by the prosecutor that the Minister of Justice had changed his death sentence to ten years imprisonment. It was only the second reprieve during Franciszek's three months in B1, whereas 120 people had been executed.

Paradoxically the three months in the condemned cell were for Franciszek the most beautiful as well as the most important in his life. He experienced a sudden conversion: "Like Saul on the road to Damascus", he recalled. In order to believe in God one has to crush all false idols. For Franciszek the concept of the righteous good man was such an idol. His belief in the righteous man had already been crushed in Auschwitz. There Franciszek realised that man's righteousness and unselfishness had definite limits. In that hell on earth, man had to become an egoist in order to survive. If he tried to help a fellow prisoner for example by sharing his bread ration, he would only speed up his own death. Why should he sacrifice his own life for someone else? A man without faith would always be tormented by the dilemma: he would feel the need for righteous and unselfish love and understand their value but again and again would realise their limits. For righteousness and unselfish love were impossible without self-sacrifice, which a man without faith would find difficult if not impossible to accept.

Franciszek arrived at B1, his beliefs crushed and with nothing to replace them. Then one day he was reading a book and came across the following passage: "God causes his sun to rise on bad men as well as good, and his rain to fall on honest and on dishonest men alike." He recognised it from his school years, yet, for the first time, he felt its true meaning. He realised the existence of the absolute and unselfish love of God for man, regardless of whether this love was accepted by man. The question of the origin of man's capacity for sacrifice on behalf of others and the meaning of such a sacrifice – which had tormented Franciszek for years – had now been answered. If we accept that we are created in the image of God then we not only can but should be prepared to give ourselves up for others. This was the only way to fulfil one's humanity. Franciszek understood Maximilian Kolbe; he also realised that had he given away his last piece of bread back in Auschwitz to a fellow prisoner, he would not have lost anything but would have become more human than ever before.

On 17 June 1961, locked up again in the same prison by the Polish communist authorities, Father Franciszek recorded in his diary, "Nineteen years ago today, I experienced the greatest day of my life. In this prison - sentenced twice – once by the people and once by myself to eternal death, I was reprieved by the decree of God's mercy. I was sitting on a stool in the corner of my cell reading a book and in particular one sentence. I experienced something extraordinary – as if someone turned on an electric switch in my soul and it was flooded by light. I recognised this light immediately. I stood up, began to pace the cell repeating to myself again and again, 'I believe, I believe.' This light has never ceased to shine in my soul, never ceased to lead me, guiding always my whole life towards God."

After his reprieve, Franciszek was taken to a prison in Racibórz. Used mainly for German prisoners, it had tolerable conditions. There was a prison chaplain there, and with the help of one of his cell mates, Franciszek became an altar-server. Not once throughout his stay in Racibórz prison did he omit the daily Mass. The well-equipped prison library contained many religious books which he now studied frantically. While he was in Racibórz prison Franciszek's mother died. He himself became seriously ill with influenza, which developed quickly in his weakened and undernourished body. When he was transferred to a camp on the German-Dutch border to work in the swamps, he was already suffering from tuberculosis. The camp doctor diagnosed that Franciszek was incapable of the hard work required. This surprising decision probably saved his life. From the camp he was sent to a prison near Zwichau, situated in the old Saxon fortress of Schloss-Osterstein. Like all the other prisoners he had to work in a nearby factory producing parts for German aeroplanes. Prisoners worked eighteen hours daily without any food, so it was not surprising that the workforce diminished rapidly.

In January 1945 the American army liberated Zwichau, just in time for Franciszek. He was on the verge of death from starvation and advanced tuberculosis. When his sister Ada arrived to take care of him, he was too weak even to travel. It was not an easy task but slowly he began to recover. There was no money and no food. Day after day Franciszek spent hours walking through the surrounding meadows in search of sorrel leaves out of which Ada would cook a soup. Every spare moment he spent in the garden reading theological books and learning Latin. He wanted to become a priest. At first he planned to go to Rome to study theology there, however both Ada and Franciszek missed the rest of the family terribly and decided therefore to return home. They took one of the first trains going east and after a week's long journey arrived in Tarnowskie Góry on 20 July 1945. His doctor insisted that Franciszek should spend at least a year resting and treating his tuberculosis. Franciszek however could not wait and, disregarding the doctor's orders, straight away entered the theological department of the Jagiellonian University in Kraków. He solemnly promised his despairing family to spend every holiday in special tuberculosis treatment hospitals and rest homes. This promise he kept and after a few years the tuberculosis was contained. However, for the rest of his life he suffered from chronic bronchitis.

2

A Young Priest in the New Socialist Poland

Franciszek was ordained in 1950 and sent to the Silesian town of Tychy as a vicar. Though young and enthusiastic he was aware that his ministry would not be very easy. With the establishment of the communist regime in Poland at the end of the war, atheism became an integral part of the new political programme. In a country where over 90% of the population were members of the well-organised Catholic Church while the membership of the Communist Party did not exceed forty thousand, programmed atheisation had to correspond to Lenin's dogma of "political compromise, zig-zags, manoeuvres of conciliation and retreat", depending on "The advance or decline of the Revolution". Nevertheless the inculcation of a scientific, or more precisely materialistic, conception of the world has not ceased to be the ultimate goal of the State throughout the post-war period. 1950 was a hard year for the Church. The postwar honeymoon period, when the new Polish government, confronted with the task of reconstructing a devastated country, had tried to appease the Church, ended with a communist "victory" in the 1947 election. With the real political opposition already crushed beforehand, the Party felt the time had come to tackle the Church. In 1950, the state took over some one thousand educational and charitable institutions administered by Caritas, keeping the name and thus confusing non-Poles who thought it was still part of the worldwide Catholic Charitable Movement. The Church press was abolished and Church property, with the exception of Church buildings and churchyards, was confiscated. "Patriotic priests' circles" were formed under pressure from the state authorities and attached to Caritas to fight the "bourgeois" hierarchy in order to destroy the unity of the Church. The Church was deprived of the right to form Catholic societies and all existing ones, along with Catholic schools, were declared illegal.

The Tychy parish was quite big even by Polish standards – some 12,000 believers. Father Franciszek was one of only two priests assigned to it and after a few months he was already tired and frustrated. He compared his work at this period to that of a farmer who kept going from field to field scattering seeds of grain with his bare hands but having no time to check what, if anything, had grown. Crowds filled the Church at each of the many Masses on Sunday. However Father Franciszek saw that most people were coming to Church more out of custom and habit than anything else. To most of his parishioners, faith was not a source of happiness and strength. Nor had it any real relevance to their lives. This religious ritualism was particularly evident among children and young people. Father Franciszek never forgot his first Sunday Mass for the parish children. As usual some two thousand packed the church and from the pulpit, raised high above the congregation, the priest was supposed to lead the liturgical responses. After a few minutes he felt more like a tamer of wild animals in a circus than a priest. "How in God's name can I summon up an atmosphere of concentration and prayer," he thought – almost panicking. At first he consoled himself with the hope of sharing his beliefs with the children during their religious instruction. However by then religious education was being forcibly abolished in schools and transferred to Church premises, and when, after several hours at school, tired children crowded into a small and unsuitable room at the vicarage, it was almost impossible to make the children listen. Father Franciszek fell into despair. He could not see how in these classes children could be led to God. He felt he was merely adding to the religious ritualism which had kept him away from God throughout his own childhood and youth.

Then he saw a chance of giving a more thorough religious education to parish altar boys. A special agreement of April 1950 between the Church and the authorities guaranteed freedom of worship. As the Mass is an integral part of worship and requires well-prepared altar boys, Father Franciszek hoped the authorities would not interfere if he formed an altar-boy group. Soon the group numbered eighty. Other priests in Poland also discovered this means of religiously instructing young boys and altar-boy groups sprang up everywhere. In some parishes there were as many as 200 altar boys. However nobody quite knew what to do with them.

Father Franciszek began to work out a "Concept

of education for altar boys". His method included theoretical spiritual guidance but also practical exercises in obedience and asceticism. He made the boys see themselves as being in the service of God – the most important of all services performed by man. Father Franciszek's methods began to prove themselves in practice. During his ministry at Tychy not once did an altar boy fail to come for his Mass even at five or six o'clock in the morning. The Diocesan Curia in Katowice became aware of his success and it was decided that he should lead the Diocesan three-day lenten retreat for altar boys.

When Father Franciszek arrived at the retreat centre, he found 120 boys, aged between ten and twelve, waiting for him in the chapel, trying in vain to sit still. He suddenly realised his task – he was meant not only to compel these fidgety beings to spend three days in silence, but also to get them to think seriously about the transience of their lives, about eternity. Father Franciszek was sure that St Ignatius, who had first thought up the idea of retreats, was a good psychologist and would never have attempted to lead spiritual exercises with children. Nevertheless, that was his task and he had to fill the next three days with something. He turned for help to his Scouting experience. He organised a bonfire, orienteering, religious hymn singing and short talks with many visual illustrations. At the end of the retreat he carried out a survey among the boys. To his surprise he found that the boys liked his retreat very much. More importantly they considered these three days to have been their deepest religious experience so far. Back in his parish, Father Franciszek critically assessed the traditional methods of organising retreats for children. He believed that they should be drastically altered in order to be meaningful. His conviction was strengthened the following year when he led another retreat for altar boys. This time 200 boys participated in it. The retreat took place at the height of the Stalinist terror. Cardinal Stefan Wyszyński, the head of the Polish Catholic Church, was under house arrest. Seven other bishops, nine hundred priests and several hundred Catholic activists had been imprisoned. A decree issued by the State Council on 9 February 1953, established the State's right to appoint and remove individual priests and bishops. Father Franciszek knew quite well that the authorities would certainly not approve of his work with the children. If discovered, at best, he would have lost his licence as a priest – at worst he would land up in prison. The Secret Police and their informers were more vigilant than ever. Poor Father Franciszek had to resort to military strategy at times to overcome obstacles and solve problems. One day he summoned the boys and told them, "The enemy is on the alert, so the 200 of us have to march through the town and meet in a nearby wood without drawing any attention to ourselves." He drew street plans and divided the boys into twos and threes. This almost military operation he managed to combine with spiritual exercises: the boys had to walk through the town in total silence and were not to look at the shop windows.

It was during this retreat that the idea of an "Oasis for the Children of God" was born. During a sermon Father Franciszek explained to the boys the meaning of a retreat. "You have been God's children since your baptism and you say 'Our Father' every day. Your life is a journey to the Father's House. On the way you get tired, sometimes lost and then you find an oasis. There you can rest, check your bearings and rethink the aim and direction of your journey."

Father Franciszek liked his idea of an "Oasis" retreat. It would give the children a model of Christian behaviour which they could follow in their daily lives. There was just one flaw. He knew that in three days one could hardly explain to the children what it really meant to be a follower of Christ – no one could expect them to remember not only the theory, but also to know how to turn it into practice. He therefore decided that the Oasis retreat must last not three days but far longer.

On 18 July 1954, Father Franciszek began the first fifteen-day Oasis retreat in Bibiela – a small village near Tarnowskie Góry. The participants were a group of about 50 altar boys from one of the Silesian parishes. Only three days later the Polish Communist authorities celebrated the tenth anniversary of "People's Poland". On 22 July 1944 the first postwar government, the Polish Committee of National Liberation (PKWN), had been formed under Soviet auspices in Lublin. Known in the West as the "Lublin Committee" it assisted its Soviet masters in administering the lands liberated from German occupation and in due course formed the core of Poland's Communist government.

Ten years of communist remodelling had left Bibiela almost unchanged and, like so many other Polish villages, it remained a Catholic stronghold. Father Franciszek and his boys stayed in an old inn which paradoxically was also used as a Communist promotion centre. A makeshift chapel was set up in a local primary school. As the Secret Police "checked" the village only rarely the local people were quite happy with this unorthodox arrangement. Father Franciszek now tried out his new programme which included time for educational activities, spiritual as well as physical exercises, and also games, thus providing for the basic needs of children between ten and fourteen years of age. In planning the Oasis retreat he had decided on a "Copernican style" change of approach. Ordinarily, a retreat leads towards confession and a resolve to try to be a better Christian. However he was not satisfied with the established approach used in parish ministry which assumed that an average Catholic usually lived in a state of mortal sin – he would go to confession to honour a religious feast, receive communion, then the next day slip back into his normal sinful state, waiting for another special occasion before receiving Christ in communion.

On his arrival in Bibiela Father Franciszek told the boys, "As Christians, we live like frogs in a swamp. From time to time we stick out our heads above its surface and breathe in some fresh clean air and then splash, back into the mire. We have to rebel against this!" he challenged the boys. "That is why here, at the 'Oasis for the children of God', we should try to live constantly as children of God so that sin and Satan are not allowed a foothold." Confession followed and then the boys were asked to try and keep a clear conscience throughout the retreat.

Father Franciszek was convinced that by and large the transmission of Catholic doctrine over the centuries had been limited to a mere educational process, like teaching any other subject. "A modern Catholic," he argued, "usually has a lot of religious knowledge. However it is a mistake to expect, in particular, children and young people, to draw the right conclusions from that knowledge and then to put it into practice in their lives." "In reality many Catholics lead a pagan life," he said. The basic principle of the Oasis retreat was therefore never to separate study from action, but to study God's word through action and to act in accordance with the knowledge acquired of God and His commandments. The main aim of the Oasis was for the boys to try as best as they could to experience the childhood of Jesus. It was expressed in the three Oasis principles – purity, obedience and love. All three were in fact contained in one principle – that of Agape, selfless love. During the fifteen days of the retreat the boys were to try to live according to Agape, overcoming their own egoism and opening themselves to the needs of others. If we truly live according to Agape, he assured the boys, then a new person, truly happy and fulfilled, develops within us.

Father Franciszek soon realised that it was impossible for one man, however energetic, to transmit a practical model of Christian life to several dozen boys. So he adopted a system, first thought out by St John Bosco, based on small groups of children with their own group leader – a slightly older boy. The leader's role was to try to show the boys a model of Christianity in practice which hopefully would remain with them. For example, one morning there was a lecture on the virtue of forgiveness. That same afternoon the boys were playing football and in the excitement one of them kicked another viciously. The victim was determined to get his own back but then the group leader intervened, "Listen, you received communion this morning", the boys nodded their heads. "Who came into your hearts?", the group leader pressed on. "Jesus", answered the boys still not quite sure what this was all about, "and you want to fight with Jesus in your hearts?" Both boys lowered their heads, then they held out their hands, smiled and simultaneously said, "I'm sorry, forgive me."

By 1957, the Oasis type of retreat had become the norm for the altar boys in the Katowice diocese and plans to hold similar retreats for girls and adults were drawn up. The following year copies of detailed instructions for Oasis type retreats were ready for distribution among the clergy if they wanted to try this new method of religious training. It soon transpired that Oasis retreats led by other priests had the same successful results as Father Franciszek's.

In the beginning of 1957 and almost by chance, Father Franciszek got involved in an anti-alcohol campaign. Six months earlier the workers of Poznań had rioted in the streets under banners proclaiming "Bread and Freedom" and "Russians go home". In the two days of fighting 53 men had died. Władysław Gomułka, who had previously been imprisoned for "nationalistic deviations", became the new Party boss. Shortly afterwards two delegates from the new leader arrived at Komańcza monastery where Cardinal Wyszyński was being held under house arrest, and asked him to return immediately to Warsaw and calm the population – he was the only person with the authority and legitimacy to be able to do so. The Church was promised the prompt release of all imprisoned priests and bishops. The decree of February 1953 on the State's right to appoint the clergy was revoked and a new agreement between the State and the Church was signed on 7 December. This gave the State the right merely to approve or veto, and not to appoint clergymen. The Church also secured the return of religious instruction in schools, the reinstatement of the Catholic press (banned in 1953), pastoral care in hospitals and prisons, and the return of the bishops removed from their dioceses by the State. For a short time the bishops even hoped for the reinstatement of some of the prewar Catholic societies, but this never came about. However five Catholic Intellectual Clubs were now allowed to exist. As a sign of the Church's hopes and a gesture of support for the new regime, Cardinal Wyszyński went to the polls in the election of 20 January 1957. The Church also agreed to cooperate with the authorities, especially in the anti-alcohol campaign – recognising widespread alcoholism as one of the most dangerous social plagues in Poland. When at the beginning of 1957 the Bishop of Katowice received an invitation from the district authorities to attend an anti-alcohol debate, he willingly delegated Father Franciszek who was, at that time, working at the Curia and in charge of the diocesan pastoral programme. Deeply disturbed by the facts and statistics on alcoholism, Father Franciszek decided that something had to be done. But what? The officially-sponsored anti-alcohol campaign, which aimed at educating Poles to drink in moderation by stressing the ill effects of excessive drinking, did not appeal to him. He strongly believed in the truth of the old saying that an alcoholic is a man who can sometimes refuse the first glass of vodka but never the second. What was needed, he thought, was to change this climate of "alcoholic terror". So Father Franciszek decided to launch a "national crusade for abstinence". Its purpose was to create small groups of people who would voluntarily abstain from

alcohol indefinitely and totally, out of Christian con-
cern and love for their brothers. They were to set an
example in their communities, slowly changing the
pattern of social behaviour throughout the country.
This voluntary abstinence, argued Father Franciszek,
was a true Crusade of the twentieth century to save
"the holy land" – man, who was degrading himself
through excessive drinking.

At first the authorities accepted and even supported
Father Franciszek's campaign. The Crusade centre was
openly established in a small wooden building near the
diocesan Curia. He was given permission to publish an
eight page anti-alcohol supplement to a Silesian Catholic weekly with a circulation of 120,000, as well as
other anti-alcohol literature. However, instead of the
eight-page supplement, soon Father Franciszek was
publishing one twice as long which he also distributed throughout Poland as an independent periodical.
Every leaflet had to be cleared beforehand with the
censor's office. Usually permission was granted for 300
to 500 copies; Father Franciszek was printing no less
than 50,000 copies of every item. The only duplicator
available was in action day and night. "There is no
time to lose," he told his helpers, numbering twenty by
now, "the authorities will close us down sooner rather
than later, but people will still have the literature."

The anti-alcohol campaign took over Father Franciszek's life and in the end, his bishop released him
from his duties at the Curia. By 1960, the Crusade
had become a national movement with over 100,000
voluntary adult abstainers, including 1,000 priests.
It enjoyed the wholehearted support of Cardinal
Wyszyński and was represented by a special priest in

each diocese who organised the Crusade locally and liaised with the National Centre in Katowice. It could also celebrate a 25% drop in the national consumption of alcohol, but despite its success its days were numbered. By 1960 internal political life had become more stable and the authorities felt strong enough to resume their ideological offensive against the Church. For the next thirteen years every "legal means", combined with administrative pressure, was used to try to lock the Church within the four walls of the sacristy. The Party programme was spelled out at a congress in March 1959 by Gomułka himself, "We do not declare war on the Church. However the Church has to remain just that – it must limit itself strictly to matters of faith, it must remain within the church's four walls." The authorities had become particularly alarmed by the dynamism of the "grass-roots" Catholic Crusade against alcohol, the first such Catholic activity since the end of the war, so they decided to crush it – despite its results. As usual, ideology took precedence over the common good.

On 29 August 1960, the work in the Crusade centre had begun earlier than usual – the last preparations for a national Crusade meeting were in progress and the atmosphere was tense. It was becoming increasingly difficult to get the censor's approval for the Crusade's literature. A recent incident involving the secret police, who had broken up a meeting of the local Crusade group, was on everybody's mind.

Father Franciszek was sitting at his desk studying papers which, because of their sensitive nature, were normally hidden away. Suddenly the door to his office swung open and his driver, a cell mate from Racibórz prison, rushed in – "Franciszek, there is going to be a search of the offices," he warned, "you'll have to hide all compromising material." Father Franciszek knew that the man, whom he trusted and regarded as a friend, was in fact also working for the security police. He just had time to warn everybody about the forthcoming ordeal when four secret police officers arrived. One of them handed Father Franciszek a document stating that the authorities had discovered that an illegal organisation, known as "The Crusade for Abstinence" was operating from the building. Father Franciszek Blachnicki, as the leader, was ordered to stop the organisation's activities immediately and to surrender all its documents. He tried to protest and showed the officers the official letter of approval he possessed. In response one of the four officers made a quick phone call and within a few minutes the entire building was surrounded by militiamen armed with guns. All documents were now systematically removed from each office despite Father Franciszek's protests. The local bishop arrived to intervene but without success. In the meantime one of Father Franciszek's helpers quickly collected the most important documents from her desk, including his memoirs and plans for developing Oasis retreats, put them into a suitcase and took it into the chapel, hoping that the search would not cover the chapel. However, one of the officers noticed her and demanded that the suitcase be brought back. On her return all four officers rushed towards the suitcase. How disappointed they were to find only a woman's clothes inside it; she left the documents hidden in the chapel. In the evening, after everything had been removed, Father Franciszek and his helpers were asked to leave the building. He refused and was removed by force. Earlier on, however, he had managed to ask one of his assistants, Ziótek, who had spent the whole day in the chapel unnoticed by the officers, to stay behind and burn the documents. That night Father Franciszek suddenly remembered that there was a bunker, dating from the war, under the building with a passage leading to the outside. He rushed through it hoping to lead out Ziótek with his papers, but when he arrived in chapel everything, including invaluable manuscripts, was already destroyed.

For Father Franciszek a period of police interrogation began. He was unrepentant and maintained that the militia's action had been illegal. Throughout Poland, the secret police were confiscating the Crusade's materials and many Crusade members had been interrogated. In October Father Franciszek went to Krościenko, a small rural town in southern Poland, at the invitation of the local parish priest. From there he sent various petitions and letters protesting against the liquidation of the Crusade to various people and State institutions. The contents of these letters, intercepted and confiscated by the authorities at the post office, later became the pretext for his arrest.

Meanwhile he tried to save the Crusade by decentralising it and continuing its work in each diocese and even at parish level. He approached Cardinal Wyszyński for help but he referred him to his Bishop. His Bishop in turn directed Father Franciszek back to the Primate. It became clear that nobody was really prepared to take the responsibility for the future of the Crusade. In the end the Bishop ordered Father Franciszek to take up a quiet post as a hospital chaplain. The Crusade was over. Father Franciszek thought this was the end of the matter but in the early spring of 1961 the interrogations were unexpectedly resumed. He was handed copies of the letters he had written in Krościenko between 25 and 27 October, together with the official prosecutor's warrant for the "confiscation of all his correspondence". The warrant was dated 15 November 1960. Father Franciszek could not believe his luck. He knew that the letters were posted on the 28 October - two weeks before the warrant. He inspected the envelopes – none had a postmark. The letters must have been picked up immediately after being posted and nobody had bothered to check the date inside. Father Franciszek accused the prosecutor of unlawful activity and lodged a formal complaint with the General Prosecutor. After four weeks a reply came back stating that the General Prosecutor's office had found his complaint unfounded as all the letters had an official postmark date of 17 November – two days after the warrant was issued. Father Franciszek knew that the authorities were determined to make a show case of him.

He was charged with the dissemination of false information, concerning the persecution of the Roman Catholic Church in Poland, to the detriment of the Polish State – which carried a possible penalty of imprisonment of up to three years. The pre-trial interrogation dragged on and on; Father Franciszek kept refusing to cooperate. Then one day he was summoned again before the prosecutor who informed him that the charge against him had been changed. Though the new charge was very similar, in this case the Penal Code prescribed a minimum sentence of three years. This meant that Father Franciszek could be arrested and detained in prison throughout the trial. He was immediately taken to the same prison where he had awaited his death sentence during the war. It was four and a half months before his trial began but for Father Franciszek this period of time at Mikołowska's prison was very happy – "a time of retreat", he once said. One day a new prisoner arrived in his cell – he was locked up for illegally producing alcohol. Surprised to find an inmate priest, he asked Father Franciszek why he was there. "I am also here because of alcohol," was the answer given to the bewildered man.

At last the trial opened in the district court of Katowice. The two main charges against Father Franciszek were the dissemination of illegal literature (of which some 200 items were listed) and of false information about the persecution of the Roman Catholic Church. The first charge was quickly dismissed when, to the fury of the judge and the joy of the courtroom audience, Father Franciszek easily proved that out of the 200 allegedly illegal items of literature, the legality of only four was in doubt. There was a particularly revealing moment when an expert from the censor's office was summoned as a witness. Every publishing house, however small, had to keep a special book in which the censor made notes during official raids as to whether the publications found had the censor's prior approval. The judge asked the expert to read out aloud the most recent notes in the Crusade's book. Father Franciszek knew that nothing illegal had been found during the raids by the censors, so he received an unexpected shock when he heard the expert say " . . . publications found were not cleared by the censor's office". Through his lawyer Father Franciszek asked the expert to read the notes again. This time he had to correct himself: "During the raid all publications found were cleared by the censors". At this the courtroom broke into laughter. As to the second charge, Father Franciszek readily agreed that he was the author of the information about the persecution of the Polish Church but he demonstrated his determination to prove the truth of his statements to the court. The judge tried to prevent Father Franciszek from giving the testimony but in the end he allowed him to take the stand. For the next few hours the court was forced to listen to a lecture on the Church and its mission. He discussed the communist concept of the Church – locked up within four walls and reduced to ritual worship – then confronted the court with his own understanding of Christianity, which apart from liturgical worship also embraced morality, education and culture. He claimed that it was because the "Crusade for Abstinence" did not fit in with the State's concept of the Church that he was standing before the court. In his summing-up speech the prosecutor ignored all the facts revealed during the trial and simply repeated the original charge of disseminating false information, demanding three years imprisonment for Father Franciszek.

The court retired to consider its verdict. The longer the court recess lasted the more Father Franciszek was sure that he would be spending the next three years in prison. At last the judge was ready to pass sentence. To the astonishment of the accused and those present in the courtroom, the judge, without any explanation changed the article under which Father Franciszek was accused – this time to one carrying a milder penalty. He then sentenced him to thirteen months imprisonment, suspended for three years. The suspended sentence, explained the judge, was due to Father Franciszek's ill-health and the fact that his activity was, after all, beneficial to society. Father Franciszek could not believe his ears. Those present in the courtroom including the official clerks, started to applaud – Father Franciszek was free.

3

From Oasis to the Light-Life Movement

After his release Father Franciszek returned to live in Krościenko, at the invitation of the parish priest and the bishop of the local diocese of Tarnów. He brought with him a group of his closest associates from the Crusade. Nobody, not even Father Franciszek, had any idea that this medieval town, so attractive to Polish mountain lovers, would become the centre of the largest religious renewal movement in Eastern Europe – one of the most interesting renewal movements to surface in the Universal Church this century. Father Franciszek enrolled at the Catholic University of Lublin where for the next two years he was researching and writing a thesis on the Oasis-type retreat as a method of Christian education of children. He decided to carry out a survey among former Oasis participants to back up his theory. Each boy was asked three questions: What do you remember from the thirty talks given during the retreat? How, if at all, was your life influenced by the retreat? What place does the Oasis retreat have in your childhood memories? Father Franciszek anxiously awaited the answers, almost regretting the idea. "What if the boys do not even remember that they were at such a retreat?" he worried. Soon the completed questionnaires began to arrive in Lublin. The answers surpassed his wildest expectations. It appeared that out of 160 boys who sent back answers, only a few remembered anything from the talks. However, in answer to the second question, the boys had compiled whole eulogies: "Since Oasis I have never skipped a daily prayer." . . . "Since Oasis I never pass a church without going inside, even if only to kneel down and make the sign of the cross." . . . "I do not drink alcohol." . . . "I do not smoke." . . . "I examine my conscience at the end of each day." . . . "I try to do at least one good deed each day." . . . "The Memory of Oasis has become a kind of Guardian Angel for me which does not let me go astray." The answers to the third question were almost unanimous. All 160 maintained that the retreat was one of the most beautiful and treasured periods of their childhood and for some also "the best summer holiday" they had ever had. Father Blachnicki was now more than ever convinced of the validity of his methods. The experience of Oasis had subconsciously made an impression on the boys and kept influencing their decisions and their way of life.

Prompted by the result of the survey, Father Blachnicki decided to revive the Oasis retreats, this time for teenagers of secondary-school age (14–18). In 1963 the first Oasis retreat for girls was organised and soon afterwards came the first "New Life Oasis" for teenage boys. The results proved even better, as the spiritual effect was deeper than in young children. The news about Oasis was spreading rapidly through the grapevine and Father Franciszek soon faced a shortage of priests who could lead Oasis retreats. Hence in 1965 the first Oasis for priests and members of religious orders was held. Father Franciszek was convinced that only through experiencing an Oasis retreat could priests fully realise its value as a method of spiritual transformation.

In 1965 the Second Vatican Council opened in Rome. The spirit of the Council and its teaching had a strong influence on the future of Oasis. Indeed in 1973, Cardinal Karol Wojtyła was to describe the Oasis movement as a translation of "the ecclesiology of the Vatican Council". The Council called upon the Church to open up to the world and to renew itself from within through the renewal of the liturgy – the source and culmination of the church's activity. This renewal was to be central to the revival of the Church in our time. The Council's vision of the liturgy was very clear to Father Blachnicki and to Oasis. After all, Oasis operated on a principle which Father Blachnicki had designated, several years before the second Vatican Council, as the best method of spiritual instruction for altar boys – that of educating for the liturgy, through the liturgy. From his own experience of Oasis Father Blachnicki knew that it was meaningful participation in the liturgy, co-creation of the liturgy, that constituted the best and surest way to a fuller understanding of the Church and one's faith. Now, strengthened and enriched by the Council's decisions to replace the Latin Mass by Mass in the national language and to revolutionise the liturgical role of the laity, Father Blachnicki worked out a new Oasis called the "Oasis of New Life", for groups of teenage boys and girls. It was then that the symbol Fos-Zoe (the Greek words for light and life) was first used in the instruction of altar servers, lectors and members of church choirs. It emphasised the unity between God's word and a life completely devoted to it. In 1969 the Oasis of New Life became an integral part of the Church's National Ministry for Liturgical Renewal. Father Blachnicki was placed in charge of introducing the new liturgy in the Polish Roman Catholic Church in accordance with the Second Vatican Council's instructions. At the same time the auxiliary bishop of Tarnów, Tadeusz Błaszkiewicz, was appointed by the Polish Episcopate to watch over Oasis and liaise between the movement and the hierarchy.

By 1969 an increasing number of Oasis members were asking for continuing spiritual instruction, between annual summer retreats, in the form of small groups within their parishes. In 1969 the first such liturgical communities of Oasis members were organised in the parishes. These groups met once a week to pray and reflect on their spiritual life in the context of the Gospel; they also became active in the liturgical renewal within the parish.

The way of life adopted by Oasis members started to influence parish life as a whole. Parishes having Oasis liturgical groups were visibly more dynamic and lively than others. The idea of the "Living Church" was emerging. This phrase proclaimed the main characteristic of the Church – that it is alive, that it resembles the Church formed by Christ as a community of believers living in unity with Christ in the Holy Spirit and building new lives together. Father Franciszek argued that despite the crowded churches at all Sunday Masses and the high percentage of children being baptised, the traditional model of the parish – an active priest with a placid flock – had little chance of long-term survival, even in Poland. "If we want the Church to be alive in our country in the 21st century, then every Polish parish must be transformed into a *Koinonia* – a Christian community based on brotherly love – a living church." Father Franciszek persuaded his closest associates of this. The building of a living church in Poland became the ultimate aim of the Oasis Movement and liturgical Oasis communities were asked to join in this effort within their parishes.

Oasis retreats, now called the "Oasis of the Living Church", spread rapidly throughout the country. In 1972 eight different types of Oasis retreats were held for various groups – children, secondary-school pupils, students, young workers, adults, seminarists, priests and nuns, following diverse programmes according to age and Christian maturity. The number of parish liturgical communities was also growing fast and a small house on the Kopia mountainside in Krościenko, acquired by Oasis in 1966, became the national centre of the movement.

This house has its own incredible story. When Father Franciszek arrived in Krościenko with a small group of his associates from the Crusade, they settled temporarily in a few rooms adjacent to the parish chapel, while looking for a place of their own. From his window Father Franciszek saw the Kopia mountain and a beautiful new house situated on its slope. "If only we could have a house like this," he wished. He shared his dream with the parish priest who told him that the house – which came with a large plot of land and forest – was in fact for sale. Its owner, Mr Kurzeja, a retired civil servant, was an unhappy and lonely man. For many years he had spent all his free time and money building this house and had hoped to retire there, far away from his wife and children, from whom he was estranged. Now, illness was forcing him to sell the house and return to Warsaw. He felt very bitter about all those years of hard work which now seemed to have been wasted. Preliminary negotiations between Father Franciszek and Mr Kurzeja began, but soon came to a halt. The price was exceedingly high, some of the money was to be paid in western currency and Mr Kurzeja also demanded a lifelong tenure in the house. Father Franciszek, brokenhearted, decided to look for a different house. However, no sooner were the negotiations broken off than Mr Kurzeja suddenly told Father Franciszek that he would like to see the house – the fruit of his life's work – in the hands of the Church, and agreed to any conditions put forward. Soon afterwards an agreement was signed and Kurzeja went to live with his family in Warsaw. After two weeks he was back – he claimed he just could not stay there a day longer. It looked as if the centre was to have a permanent lodger but after a few weeks Mr Kurzeja was taken to hospital. Advanced lung cancer was diagnosed. In the hospital he decided to make his confession – for the first time in many years. He died soon after, on the feast of the Resurrection, contented in the knowledge that his life's work would not go to waste.

Every year an extension was added to the house (though without official state permission) and yet the centre still became more and more crowded. There was no space to hold large meetings; the existing parish chapel was also too small for such requirements. In 1973, in anticipation of the tenth anniversary of the Oasis retreats, Father Franciszek decided to improve the space problem. That spring, the construction of a wooden building to hold 120 people began (again without permission from the authorities). It was named "The Tabernacle of Light". Its twelve walls and an enormous lamp made out of coloured glass (some 400 kilograms in weight) symbolised the New Jerusalem of the Book of Revelation. Nearby a "Spring of Life" was created. The water from the spring flowed in a narrow meandering channel alongside which were placed wooden benches engraved with Bible quotations. A three-metre high statue of Mary, Mother of the Church, stood at the foot of the spring. It was here, on 11 June 1973, that Cardinal Karol Wojtyła, the future Pope John Paul II, dedicated the Living Church movement to Mary, Mother of God.

1973 was an important year for the Living Church movement. It was then that the formal structure of the whole movement at the parish, diocese and national level was established. At the same time a detailed programme of spiritual instruction which remains in force to this day, was drawn up for the whole year. It was divided into three parts – Oasis summer retreats, post-Oasis activity during the school year and pre-Oasis preparation. A new type of Oasis was introduced. It consisted of several smaller units for children, young people and adults. Each small unit had its own independent programme though all the units would come together to hold a united meeting to fully experience being part of a community of believers and to share their spiritual transformation. In between the summer retreats spiritual development was continued in small groups meeting once a week for prayer and bible study. Every six or seven weeks a communal day was organised at diocesan level. In the summer of 1973 the first Oasis retreats for families were also organised. As a result family communities of the Living Church were set up. The family movement, existing as part of the whole Living Church movement, became known as the Home Church. Since 1973, during the vigil of Pentecost, representatives of all Oasis groups throughout the country have come to Krościenko to take part in the so called "Mother Oasis"; they are given detailed instructions for the summer retreats together with all necessary teaching aids. During a special service those who are to lead the retreats receive a special blessing and are given Oasis candles, symbolising unity by being lit from one central candle which remains in Krościenko. These candles are used by every group during its services throughout the summer.

Between 1973 and 1976 the movement grew rapidly; the numbers of people participating in the summer retreats and the post-Oasis programme trebled from 7,000 to 20,000, while the number of family groups in the Home Church grew from 51 to 157. By 1976 the idea of the Living Church began to influence different groups within the Polish Church as well as the clergy and hierarchy. Among the bishops, Cardinal Karol Wojtyła very soon became one of the best friends and patrons of the movement. Since 1970 he had regularly visited the summer retreats, usually on "Community Days".

Volumes could be written about the links between the movement and the present Pope – the memory of one was particularly treasured by Father Franciszek. It was 16 August 1972, the Community Day on Mount "Tabor" – as Oasis members called the beautiful Błyszcz mountain, 833 metres above sea level and situated in the Beskid Sądecki range in the south of Poland. 25 Oasis groups, some 700 people, plus a large crowd of local residents, were waiting for Cardinal Wojtyła. He was to come from the direction of the valley accompanied by his chaplain and a small group of Oasis guides. On the way up, the Cardinal, dressed in a tourist outfit, looked at the rapidly gathering clouds in the sky, heard the wind bellowing through the adjacent wood and the rising rumble of thunder in the distance. "I know three madmen," the Cardinal joked, "the first is myself, the second is my chaplain and the third is waiting for us at the summit." The third madman – Father Franciszek – came out to meet the Cardinal and together they climbed the last part of the route. One of the priests present took a photograph: "Treat it with care, one day this photograph will be worth a fortune in the West," the Cardinal jested. Soon he was ready to concelebrate Mass with some 50 Oasis priests, who surrounded an altar built out of a huge pile of rocks. The sky was overcast with dark clouds by the time the Cardinal finished his short sermon; he quickly glanced at the sky and turned to Father Franciszek and asked, "Shall we stop and climb down to the church in the valley?" "It will pass by," was the reply. No sooner had the liturgy of the Eucharist begun than the thunder cracked and the rain poured. The congregation closed ranks tightly. The sound of hymns mingled with the thunder claps. Gusts of wind blew out the candles; the altar was now lit only by recurrent lightning flashes. Only two umbrellas were to be found among those present – barely enough to keep the rain away from the centre of the altar. The storm subsided with the end of the Mass. Father Franciszek did not dare to test his weather predictions any more and decided that the programme would continue in the church in the valley – the walk would help dry out their clothes at the same time. In the shelter of the church, with over 700 lighted candles held aloft by all present, the hour of witness began; people of all ages and walks of life spoke openly and unashamedly about their inner spiritual transformations.

"More than ever I was made aware of God's infinite, inexpressible love for humanity. Only the person who possesses a portion of this love can understand his neighbour and genuinely forgive him." . . . "I appreciated the fellowship most of all. Oasis restored my faith in people – in their goodness and selflessness. I was also impressed by the way the young men and women related to each other. Friendships were warm and considerate; something which has become unusual these days" . . . "Oasis has led to a change in my life and my behaviour. I want to join a group in which we can study the Bible together" . . . "I want Jesus to become my way" . . . "None of us expected much from the Oasis retreat. We came loaded with problems to which we had not been able to find answers. We usually kept our distance from the so-called Christian way of life. We had chosen the easier way, accepting the deceptive values of today's declining civilisation. Here at the retreat we have seen a way of life based on inner conviction, which springs from meditation on Christ's teaching." . . . "While we were standing for prayer I very much wanted the others to pray for me, but my shyness prevented me from making this request. So I asked God to give me boldness . . . and after a few moments I was able to ask the group. I was so happy when they prayed for me. I was glad that I had finally been able to express my needs in words – that day I truly believed in God, which is the most important thing of all." . . . "These two weeks of retreat have given me more than eight years of religious classes. I always felt that something was missing. Here I was able to find it . . . in the school of prayer. I drew near to God." . . . "In a way I came as an observer. I wanted to see what it was all about, to form my own opinion of Oasis. Now I am convinced I want to tell people about Christ wherever I am." . . . "I felt so close to the Church. It seemed as if God had allowed me to attain the gift of His goodness and love. My heart is overflowing with joy." . . . "At Oasis I discovered who Jesus really is and what a central role He can play in my life. Here I have learnt to love not only God, but my neighbour as well. I know now how to pray to God." . . . "I came to Oasis almost by mistake, thinking it was to be an ordinary summer camp. I must say I have never met young people like those in my Oasis group. Suddenly daily Mass ceased to be a 'penance' or a 'tedious duty' for me and became the best hour of each day – my direct contact with God in communion. Now I want to go to sow the seed not where the Oasis atmosphere already exists but where nobody has heard of Oasis."

"I simply cannot express my gratitude to my parish priest who advised me to take part in the Oasis retreat. Here I took a look at my life, at its meaning. I value most my discovery of Agape – the true love. This one word contains within itself so much: mature love, overcoming egoism, limitless service to others. It might mean paying a high price but it gives in return a true happiness. It teaches us to see Christ in others." "Oasis is one of the most beautiful pastoral activities of our Church. The Church in Poland would be one brotherly community if all believers lived in accordance with the ideals of Oasis. These ideals must enrapture Christians who want to lead a truly Christian life . . . Here I experienced brotherly love and unity. I am so glad I have met so many people who want to live in accordance with the teaching of the Gospel. During Mass I become aware that as a responsible member of the living Church I have to live Christ every day of my life and to show him to others." . . . "The teachings of the retreat helped me greatly. For the first time I realised just how great God is, how much He loves us and what He expects from us. Therefore I resolved to overcome my faults, with which I have always had trouble, to discipline myself and live for Him."

The Cardinal, visibly touched by these testimonies, joined us with his own which clearly showed his appreciation of the movement and the importance he attached to it. "This afternoon gave me so much satisfaction. Most of all because your way of life is so clear to me. I tried to live it too in the past, together with your parents. Only then it was not so mature and deep . . . or so much in the spirit of the Second Vatican Council. Today when I look at you, at Oasis, I can clearly see how much the Council's vision of the Church has penetrated your retreats and your lives. I cannot express how much joy this gives me as a bishop for whom the Council and its vision of the Church have become the central theme of life. I look at you from the perspective of the struggle taking place in our country, a struggle for a way of life, for a system of values, for the largely spiritual values of our youth. Our future depends on you. There are so many of you today. I think that during the Oasis retreat, each of you can create an Oasis within yourself before returning to the desert which surrounds us . . . and I wish that every one of you could become such an Oasis, for then the desert would no longer be dangerous."

In March 1976 the first congress for Oasis leaders took place in Krościenko. Since then it has become an annual event during which the leaders of the movement assess the work of the previous year and outline their future programme. At this time, Father Franciszek was determined to change the name of the movement. He agreed with some critics that the name of "The Living Church" could be interpreted as suggesting that the parishes outside the movement's influence represented only the dead part of the church. Those present at the congress were divided into ten groups and given two hours to think out a new name for the movement which would best represent its essence, programme and methods. All ten names were handed to Father Franciszek at the beginning of an afternoon session. He took the first piece of paper and read out aloud, "Light–Life", then the second, "Light–Life"; all ten groups had arrived at exactly the same name. Father Franciszek was visibly moved; he did not believe this unanimity was a mere coincidence. To him it was the best proof that the Holy Spirit was guiding the movement. So it was that during the first congress at Krościenko the Greek signs of Fos and Zoe (Light and Life) became the symbols of the movement. Light must become life; there can be no gulf between that which is recognised as principle and that which is professed as an attitude to life. The light which is to become life is the light of God's word, the light transmitted to mankind as Lumen Gentium. The aim of the movement was clearly formulated – all members, regardless of their age and status in the Church should strive towards Christian maturity through God's word, the liturgy and prayer; through witness and service in the community.

Prior to the congress in Krościenko Father Franciszek had closely studied a programme of evangelisation in the modern world, announced by Pope Paul VI to mark the tenth anniversary of the Second Vatican Council. In it Paul VI argued that if the Church is to be constantly renewed, evangelisation must continue within the Church, linked to the process of renewal. Pope Paul VI reminded believers that the church was the fruit of evangelisation by Jesus and his 12 apostles, and an extension of their mission. That was why the community of Christians should preach the Good News through word and witness not only to those who do not know Christ but also to those who claim to believe in Him, so that first their conscience may be transformed, then their actions, and in the end their entire life – thus creating a new person. The new person should in turn form small, intimate Christian communities which would radiate Christian values with the ultimate aim of forming a future Christian society where a new, deeply Christian culture would prevail. However, Pope Paul VI underlined that the Church has to continuously evangelise itself if its apostolic dynamism and conviction are to be maintained. Father Franciszek had tried to analyse the reasons why some Oasis parish groups showed worrying signs of forming closed communities, in a sense looking down on the rest of the parish. He realised that these people had not met Christ or formed a personal relationship with him in the Holy Spirit. He concluded that meeting Christ and establishing a personal relationship with Him was an absolutely necessary stage in the formation of a mature Christian – one which could not be missed out. Father Franciszek put forward a new programme of evangelisation for every member of the movement. A new type of Oasis retreat was introduced which involved training baptised Christians to confirm their absolute willingness to bear witness to Christ and accept all the consequences of their faith. It was designed as a three-year programme, involving three stages of Christian maturity – (1) meeting Christ and the conscious acceptance of Him as Lord and Saviour, (2) renewal of baptismal vows and (3) bearing witness to Christ in the community.

The programme was to be carried out during the summer retreats and during the post-Oasis period within the parish community. A new system of recruiting people for summer camps was adopted. Everyone who wished to participate in an Oasis retreat had to fulfil a special programme of individual evangelisation or to take part in an evangelistic retreat in their parish. It was stressed that the parish retreat could take place only in parishes where the resident priest had carefully studied and accepted the programme of parish revival and carried it out in cooperation with the movement.

In Father Franciszek's plans, the evangelisation of each member of the movement was just the beginning. According to the Church's own data, some half a million young people in Poland had never heard the Good News or received even a minimal religious education –

they had little or no contact with the Church. Father Franciszek also knew that the traditional forms of popular religion, the only kind allowed by the authorities, produced "practising believers" who would fulfil the minimum of religious duties, but without developing a mature faith or the ability to bear witness to Christ as part of daily life. However, under the conditions of official repression of Christianity, the harsh reality was that only a person who was prepared to share his faith with others could keep it himself. To deal with this problem the Polish church, since 1956, had undertaken a number of attempts at active Christianisation alongside more traditional Church activities. University chaplaincies, five Catholic Intellectuals' clubs and Christian culture weeks all formed part of the church's limited offensive. Now the Light-Life movement was to embark on a mission to evangelise the whole of Polish society through its small but dynamic groups within each parish. It was to take Christ and His teachings not only to those who had never heard about Him, but also to those who had heard about Jesus but did not accept him as their Lord and Saviour. Father Franciszek argued that as the Light-Life movement's aim was to help every person to reach Christian maturity, evangelisation was not only its natural consequence but also the best proof of its authenticity.

4

We Have One Father in Heaven

By the mid-1970s rumours about the Catholic renewal movement developing in "communist" Poland had begun to filter through to the West. The movement's vision of a pastoral ministry which emphasised living faith based on a personal relationship with Christ as well as Bible study, prayer, worship and personal testimony, aroused immediate interest among Western Protestants. They began to descend on Krościenko, on fact-finding missions, both as individuals and as groups. Protestant Christians from outside Poland began attending and participating in Oasis retreats, sharing their own religious experiences. All were welcomed wholeheartedly. Ever since the Second Vatican Council committed the Roman Catholic Church to the ecumenical movement and put forward the reunion of all Christians as one of the Church's main aims, Father Franciszek had been searching for a way to educate the movement's members in the spirit of ecumenism. Specific Polish conditions made this task rather difficult. Despite a joint commission of the Polish Ecumenical Council (made up of the eight largest Christian churches) and the Episcopal commission for ecumenical work, and the weeks of prayer for Christian unity organised annually in every diocese, unofficial ecumenical encounters and cooperation outside these rigid formalities had been very rare in Poland.

In the mid-1970s when the Light-Life movement identified itself with the worldwide movement of Catholic charismatic renewal, some contacts developed between Oasis and Polish Pentecostals – but these were very cautious and sporadic. Occasionally other individual Polish Protestants participated in Oasis retreats or prayer circles but on the whole the Polish Protestant churches preferred to keep away from the movement. In a country where the total number of Protestants does not exceed 100,000 in comparison to 30 million Catholics, Polish Protestants had reason to distrust a dynamic Catholic renewal movement, which had already proved attractive to young Poles. There was also another problem. The Roman Catholic Church was the theological, ecclesiastical and cultural womb in which Oasis and the Light-Life movement were formed. Although the movement extended the church's sphere of pastoral ministry in various ways, this has not been at the expense of traditional piety. Polish Catholicism's proverbial devotion to the Virgin Mary has been retained and cultivated within the movement. This strong Marian overtone was of course indigestible to the Polish Protestants. However, there was another problem. As small, non-Catholic bodies, the Polish Protestant churches receive a number of concessions from the State authorities and are often seen by Catholics as dependent on

State favours. In this context the reserve of Polish Protestants to get involved with the Light-Life movement was interpreted by many within the movement as reluctance to risk the disapproval of the State authorities.

To Western Protestants Father Blachnicki's model of faith, conceived as individual encounter with Christ and total trust in Him, as well as the emphasis put on Bible studies by the Light-Life movement, were a revelation. For a time it was even thought by some that the movement was more Protestant than Catholic. Ecumenical encounters cooled down a little when the strictly Catholic features of the movement, such as its devotion to the cult of Mary and its unity with the established Roman Catholic Church became more clear. The movement left many Protestants baffled by its complex inner dynamics, standing solidly within Polish Catholicism and yet surging, pioneer fashion, across all its traditional boundaries. It also challenged some individual religious prejudices. "Is it a spiritual phenomenon or a socialist mutation; a glowing ember or a flash in the pan," demanded a young American Protestant on returning from a visit to Krościenko.

After 1976 the centrality of evangelism in the Oasis programme led Father Blachnicki to establish contacts with Protestant evangelistic groups including "Campus Crusade for Christ" – an American-based interdenominational movement known also as "Agape", which pursues evangelistic activities in over 80 countries throughout the world with real success. Agape concentrates on preaching the basic Christian truths common to all denominations and aims at helping individuals to establish a personal relationship with Jesus, accepting Him as Christ the Saviour and Lord. Those who become believers are then encouraged to join a local church of their choice in order to continue their spiritual growth through further instruction within the local Christian community. Agape's aims fitted in perfectly with Father Franciszek's ideas of the best way to introduce young people to the movement and its secondary training programme. Agape's simple but effective methods, its evangelical talks based on the Bible, appealed to Father Blachnicki. He was also very impressed with the movement's dynamism, eagerness to preach the Gospel and readiness to adopt their programmes to suit denominational and local religious tradition.

In 1975 he decided on an unprecedentedly close form of cooperation with Campus Crusade for Christ in his programme for the evangelisation of Poland. In the summer of 1976 representatives of the Agape movement arrived in Poland at the invitation of Father Blachnicki, to lead special evangelisation sessions at several of the Oasis retreats. Since 1977 Agape members have been participating in the New Life Oasis – run according to a new evangelistic programme. In 1978 Agape members were also invited to run prayer circles and to give instruction on the methodology of evangelisation during Oasis retreats for group leaders. In an Institute for Evangelisation set up by Father Franciszek, delegates from both movements worked on preparing new programmes for evangelisation which would be relevant to Polish conditions, as well as suitable visual aids. In the late 1970s, "Youth with a Mission" – another American based evangelistic movement, became actively involved in Father Blachnicki's programme for evangelisation – mainly by preparing group leaders.

Father Franciszek's down-to-earth cooperation with

non-Catholic movements as well as his enthusiasm for such cooperation alarmed the more conservative sections of the Catholic clergy and the Episcopate. Father Franciszek was accused of trying to protestantise the movement. A lengthy memorandum, "Notes concerning manifestations of Baptist infiltration of the Roman Catholic Church through the Light-Life movement" by a Jesuit priest called Zbigniew Frarzkowski was widely circulated in Poland. Rumour had it that even Cardinal Wyszyński was worried about this "Protestant penetration". A special Church commission was set up to investigate the accusations. Among its appointed members were Bishop Władysław Miziołek (the chairman of the commission for Ecumenism) and Cardinal Karol Wojtyła of Kraków. During a day-long enquiry Father Blachnicki defended himself by appealing to official church documents such as Pope Paul VI's exhortation on evangelisation *Evangelii Muntiandi* and the Decree on Ecumenism of the Second Vatican Council, which had given tacit approval for ecumenical cooperation. Father Franciszek quoted Pope Paul VI, "We make our own the desire of the Fathers of the Third General Assembly of the Synod of Bishops for a collaboration marked by a greater commitment with the Christian brethren with whom we are not yet in perfect unity, taking as a basis the foundation of Baptism and the patrimony of faith which is common to us. By doing this we can already give a greater common witness to Christ before the world in the very work of evangelisation. Christ's command urges us to do this, the duty of preaching and of giving witness to the Gospel requires this."

Father Franciszek claimed that it was in this close

cooperation between the Light-Life movement and the Campus Crusade for Christ that the appeal of the "Vatican Council's Fathers" was being fulfilled. "Catholics must joyfully acknowledge and esteem the truly Christian gifts of our common heritage which are to be found among our separated brethren. It is right and salutory to recognise the riches of Christ and the virtuous works in the lives of others who are bearing witness to Christ, sometimes even by shedding their blood. For God is always wonderful in His works and worthy of admiration. Nor should we forget that whatever is wrought by the Grace of the Holy Spirit in the hearts of our separated brethren can contribute to our own edification. Whatever is truly Christian never conflicts with the genuine interests of the faith, indeed it can always result in a more ample realisation of the very mystery of Christ and the Church."

At the end of the day's meeting all charges contained in the memorandum were dismissed by the Commission. Moreover Cardinal Wojtyła praised the Light-Life movement for its contribution to the renewal of the Polish Church while Bishop Miziołek stressed that the ecumenical contacts of the Light-Life movement were not only tolerable, but should be cultivated in accordance with the directives of the Second Vatican Council, Pope Paul VI and the Polish Episcopate. In a special letter Bishop Miziołek informed all Polish diocesan bishops of the outcome of the inquiry.

This official acquittal was not enough for Father Blachnicki. He was worried, quite justifiably, that not even all the long-standing members of the movement fully understood the significance of the cooperation between the Light-Life movement and Agape in their evangelistic endeavour. As a consequence he decided that the issue of ecumenism would be the leading topic of lectures and discussions at the forthcoming Fifth Annual National Congress of the movement's 700 leaders.

Among various lectures delivered at the Congress was one by Father Franciszek himself on the methods of ecumenical dialogue. In the context of the recommendation for Ecumenism made by the Second Vatican Council and ecumenical pronouncements of John Paul II he assessed the current state of ecumenism worldwide. He pointed out that in the short period since the Second Vatican Council more had been done to restore Christian unity than over many previous centuries. Countless ecumenical commissions and institutions had been set up, ecumenical journals published, and weeks of prayer for Christian unity organised. Despite all these encounters the ecumenical movement was now in an impasse, claimed Father Franciszek, limited to intellectual dialogue and superficial ecumenical encounters.

Reiterating the vision of ecumenism put forward by the Second Vatican Council, Father Blachnicki argued that this was because attempts at Christian unity had become separated from the process of renewal of the Church and evangelism. He contended that the more we strive to live according to the Gospel, the more we are fostering and even practising Christian unity at the highest level in the Spirit. The usual difficulties which cropped up in ecumenical encounters – the different language used to describe the same experiences, varied emphasis, and neglect of particular Christian traditions, could be overcome by a spirit of cooperation and mutual sharing which highlighted points of agreement. Analysing the cooperation between the Light-Life movement and Agape in the field of evangelisation, Father Franciszek made everybody present aware of the strong spiritual bond between the two, which had developed along the way – a bond which should be seen as a small contribution towards the future unity of all Christians. Group discussions followed Father Blachnicki's lecture; all were asked to make their own assessment of the contacts between Agape and the Light-Life movement. The overwhelming majority recognised with gratitude the valuable contribution of Agape to the movement's evangelistic programme.

Equally appreciated was the material assistance offered to the Light-Life movement by its Western friends. Indeed some two million copies of the Polish Bible had been printed outside Poland, paid for by Western Protestant churches and groups and then handed over to the movement. These included twelve baskets full of Bibles handed over to "Light-Life" by Pope John Paul II during his first trip to Poland in June 1979. Publication of Bibles and religious literature in Poland had been severely restricted due partly to the lack of funds but mainly to the deliberate policy of the Polish State Authorities. It was not until 1965 that the Church was allowed to print the first few thousand Bibles since the end of the war. Not surprisingly the gift of over two million Bibles was received with enormous gratitude by the Polish Catholics. However, arguably the most touching example of Ecumenism at work came in the summer of 1981. Some 45,000 young people applied to attend Oasis retreats that summer – the last summer of the "Official Solidarity" era. The country had already been plunged into economic chaos which was mostly engineered from the top but blamed on Solidarity. The shops were empty and people queued for hours to obtain basic food including bread. Solidarity was, needless to say, blamed for all shortages by the state controlled media; in stage-managed interviews seemingly ordinary citizens denounced the free trade union and called for tough government action. Food rationing was introduced and Oasis, treated as "illegal camps" by the authorities, could not buy food. Some faint-hearted participants argued that under such circumstances the summer retreats should be cancelled. Father Franciszek would not hear of this. He immediately appealed for help to the West. Soon eleven trucks, each carrying twenty tons of food, arrived in Poland. They came from Austria, Norway, Denmark and France. In Norway, the twelve different branches of the country's Protestant Church cooperated together for the first time since the Reformation to run a very successful and united Oasis campaign. Thanks to the generosity of Western Christians the Oasis retreats were saved.

5

Christianity for Saints

"At the heart of our whole movement is the courage of faith; the courage to demand of everyone a genuine Christian faith", Father Franciszek once said. "When we priests face children and young people either as pastors or as teachers of religion, we are afraid that they have not grown up enough to understand what we tell them about God. Then we resort to different psychological, pedagogical and sociological tricks. It seems as if our pastoral care is, to a great extent, a social technique, a search for different means in order to catch people, to attract them and bind them to something. Meanwhile children and young people are waiting for the authentic Word of God, for the authentic Gospel. Young people expect that great effort will be demanded from them. So we should not be afraid to set high standards and to preach the one true Gospel. We should not preach a double set of morals: one for average normal Christians and another for the chosen, who are called to be saints, to live their lives in accordance with the Gospel. There should be just one model of Christian life which should be offered to all." It was this model of authentic and demanding Christianity, "Christianity for Saints", that Father Blachnicki offered first to young Polish boys and girls and later to the entire population.

The Light-Life movement's vision of pastoral ministry emphasises a living faith based on a personal relationship with Christ as one's Saviour, strengthened and matured through the study of the Bible. This is the guide to a new life, through prayer-conversation with Christ based on His own words and those of the Liturgy – especially the Eucharist. Father Franciszek strongly believed that a personal relationship with Christ has to develop within a small Christian community which in turn is a part of the entire Church – the community of all Christians. Hence spiritual development takes place in small groups led by a trained group leader – an "animator". "If the relationship with Christ exists on this level then witness and mission are natural, unavoidable consequences", Father Blachnicki claimed.

At the heart of the entire spiritual formation of the Light-Life movement are the Oasis retreats. In essence Oasis represents a unique method of encounter in the Holy Spirit, among believers, through the profession and practice of their faith. All elements of Oasis are directed towards this goal – leading to a personal encounter with Christ, in the Holy Spirit, through the community of the church which is present in every basic Oasis group. This personal encounter with Christ during Oasis retreats, experienced by hundreds of thousands of young Poles, has already been regarded by Father Franciszek as the basic charisma given to the movement by God.

In 1986 some sixteen programmes of intensive Christian formation, varying according to Christian maturity, age, profession and apostolic calling, were carried out in Oasis retreats – mostly in the summer. These included: Oasis for the children of God, Oasis for a new life (three stages), Oasis for students and working youth, Oasis for families (three stages), Oasis for priests, seminarians, nuns and catechetical instructors, Oasis for Evangelisation, Oasis for group leaders, Oasis for "animators" in charge of evangelisation programmes and Oasis for the diaconate of liberation. In addition, several other types of retreats are organised through the year for group leaders and priests; there is also a special Oasis for prayer which was first started in 1977. Several Oasis for prayer groups are organised simultaneously in various places through Poland. They last 48 hours – from Friday evening until Sunday night – and offer participants the possibility of learning to pray better. All kinds of prayer are used during the retreat, from liturgical prayer, through meditation and intercession, to adoration: everyone is welcome at this type of Oasis. The usual Oasis summer camp consists of 60-80 people, though very large camps are becoming more and more popular. All participants in every Oasis are divided into groups of between eight and ten people, each led by an "animator", often only a few years older than the rest of the group. The responsibility for the entire camp lies with a priest called a "moderator".

Though different in detail, the fifteen day programme always follows one pattern: each day begins with communal prayer as early as 7 a.m., followed by Mass. The sermon corresponds to one of the fifteen mysteries of the Rosary, to which the whole day is then dedicated.

After Mass and a meagre breakfast there is an hour of group work "sharing the Gospel". Extracts from the Bible are read and discussed under the supervision of the "animator". Emphasis is put on the relevance of Christ's teaching to the everyday life of Oasis members. Then there is a break for lunch and a free period which allows time for personal prayer, meditation and reading. The group meets again in the early afternoon for an "open-eyed walk" through the surrounding countryside. The idea of the walk is to intensify awareness of the beauty and perfection of nature and point to the Creator of all things, God, while contrasting this with the abuse of God's gifts by man.

In the late afternoon all groups meet together for "Bible School" – a theological lecture delivered by a priest. The day ends with a bonfire; everyone sings contemporary religious hymns. The singing is interrupted from time to time by a spontaneous meditation or a prayer. The day ends with a communal prayer at about ten o'clock.

There are three exceptions to this pattern. On the fourth day, the offertory day, a liturgy is held for the renewal of baptismal vows. By the single gesture of lighting a small candle from a huge common candle the participants pledge themselves to follow the true Light – Christ. On the ninth day the Way of the Cross is acted out. A huge cross, corresponding to the original size, is carried in turn by the participants. At the twelfth station a Mass is celebrated at a makeshift altar. Whenever possible a hill is chosen for the Way of the Cross to add to the physical realism. The thirteenth day is "Pentecost Day", also called Community Day. Several camps come together for the day, sometimes with as many as a thousand people or more. During a solemn Mass representatives from all camps share their spiritual experiences. On the last evening before departure, instead of the usual simple evening meal, there is an Agape banquet, a traditional Christmas supper (lavish by Oasis standards), for all participants. Agape ends with an hour of witness – people pray openly about the meaning and importance to them of the last fifteen days. Next morning the last Mass is celebrated and all participants are "sent" out into the world to spread the good news, as the Apostles were sent by Christ.

During the fifteen days of the retreat all participants, whether schoolboys or priests, try to grasp more fully the meaning of "new life" in Christ, establishing a closer communion with God through Jesus Christ in the Holy Spirit. "Nobody is born as a Christian," Father Franciszek once explained, "we have to become better Christians every day of our lives by confirming our willingness to profess Christ at any given moment and in any situation, to reject and overcome our weakness, sometimes in a long process of painful internal struggle, so that in the end others might see God in us." Oasis was always seen by Father Franciszek as a start to the long process of becoming a mature Christian. Within its whole programme of spiritual development, Oasis has been giving every participant a model of truly Christian life. An important feature of the retreat has been that Christian principles are not simply taught but lived out – that a prayer-relationship with God is not separated from everyday duties and endeavours, however small and trivial they may seem. After all, our life consists of small matters even though it is not a small matter in itself.

Between summer retreats all individuals are expected to continue their spiritual growth within the same basic group following one of many post-Oasis programmes. These are based on a weekly group meeting led by an animator. As with Oasis retreats the diverse programmes are carried out according to one pattern. Every meeting allows for "verification of one's life" – assessing an aspect of one's life in the light of Christ's teaching. There is also Bible reading followed by a discussion as well as communal prayer. The only exception to this rule is the yearly programme of development for family circles. Deeply impressed by the spiritual development of married couples in the French based "Equipes de Notre Dame" movement, Father Blachnicki decided to import its methods and use them for the formation of family circles within the Light-Life movement. Monthly meetings are organised for each family circle led by a couple acting as animators, under the supervision of a local parish priest. The three-hourly meeting is divided into four parts. After a modest supper, communal prayer leads to "sharing the Gospel". An extract from the Bible is read and discussed, individuals ask everyone to pray for special intentions; sometimes the group recites the rosary together. Then one of seven topics is discussed: community, prayer, mutual spiritual life, selflessness, marriage dialogue, marriage prayer, or the Christian rules of life. A task is given out connected with the main topic – for example during a weekly meeting when marriage prayer has been discussed, all couples commit themselves to pray together every day. At the end all share their experience of fulfilling commitments made at the previous meeting. The evening ends with a communal prayer. It usually takes 3 years for an average family circle to work through all 7 topics. Then articles from "Home Church" – a Light-Life periodical – are used as subjects for group discussions. In time, step by step, couples commit themselves to daily reading of the Bible and daily prayer – individually, with a marriage partner and with the children, trying to overcome all shared and common weaknesses such as gossiping, ill temper and bad time-keeping, as well as maintaining the marriage dialogue. This dialogue is treated as a religious act – once a month husband and wife sit down together and in the presence of God they examine their marriage with all its problems, trying to understand God's plan in relation to themselves. Often a third chair is placed in a prominent place to help the couple to remember that this intimate conversation is taking place between three parties. In time the couples are expected to form new family circles though continuing their spiritual growth within their original group.

Everyone agrees that recruitment to Oasis retreats, at first, was rather haphazard. Some people knew exactly what they were looking for at Oasis – like the young couple who came the day after their wedding to spend their honeymoon at the retreat. "So that we could start a truly new life together", they explained to the nun in charge of their group. Others came out of curiosity or followed a friend. Some, persuaded by their parish priest to take the opportunity of cheap holidays in the more beautiful parts of Poland, were shocked on their arrival. Living conditions have changed little over the years – they are still spartan. Participants lodge with local farmers, often sleeping in barns. Shopping and preparing meals is done by each of the participants on a daily rota system. Meals are usually eaten outdoors regardless of the weather. The diet is based on bread and margarine, with jam considered as a treat. The group on duty also has the washing up to do. Some protested "Why should we work? We paid for a holiday after all." There were some people who left on the first day. The vast majority remained and after a few days the spirit took over from the body and the Oasis became more like a loving family.

Over the years a detailed system of spiritual development has been worked out and all those who come to their first Oasis of New Life have received evangelisation either through individual contact with one of many Oasis group leaders or in a parish retreat, along with a period of post-evangelisation work within a small group. This period aims at helping every member to experience a personal encounter with Christ and accept Him as Lord and Saviour. During the weekly meetings of the post-evangelisation period which are run by a trained animator all members of the small group are initiated into their new life as followers of Christ. The post-evangelisation period ends with The Oasis of New Life.

The aim of the first stage of the Oasis of New Life is to awaken in the participants the desire to become part of the community of Christ's followers and to begin a systematic spiritual development within a three-year period. There are weekly formation meetings following a special programme. In the first year ten topics are chosen for discussion which are intended to help every individual to grasp essential aspects of the faith. These are seen as ten steps towards Christian maturity: Jesus Christ, the Virgin Mary, the Holy Spirit, the Church,

God's Word, Prayer, the Liturgy, Witness, the New Culture and Agape. Between meetings all members of the group follow a daily routine of meditation, Bible reading and prayer, according to a specially prepared notebook. In addition the group works through a ten-week programme of introduction to the Bible as the history of salvation. After the first year, development concentrates on in-depth understanding of the sacraments and the liturgy. Throughout the year weekly discussions concentrate on God's word within the context of the liturgical year. The whole group experience Easter and the feast of Pentecost together in one of the Oasis retreat centres. The third year programme aims to grasp the mystery of the Church as a community of believers and to pledge willingness to use one's God-given gifts. Until martial law was imposed on 13 December 1981, the third stage Oases took place in Rome – the heart of Catholicism. As part of its many restrictions on civil liberty, martial law limited travelling abroad to a minimum, so a decision was taken to organise the third stage Oases in Poland. At this stage, all members of the group enter the last period of the growth cycle – the preparation for some kind of service in the diaconate within the movement and the local community.

In one of his lectures Father Franciszek pointed out, "There have been so many beautiful and sound pastoral plans to revive the Church, but all remain just that – plans which have not been transformed into reality. The fundamental mistake of all these plans is that they merely put forward goals, forgetting about the methods and the people who should be trained to implement a beautiful plan in the world. Theory alone cannot create life. Life is born only from life. Only people captured by an idea and in possession of an effective means of action can save life, can make it bloom and prosper." Hence all the different diaconates which exist in the movement:– the diaconate for liberation, the diaconate for evangelism, the diaconate for training, the diaconate for the liturgy, the diaconate for the "Home Church" and the diaconate which contains within itself all the others – the diaconate for parish community.

No matter what diaconate Oasis members undertake, they are expected to continue their spiritual growth with their original group as well as themselves becoming evangelists within their own environments. Evangelisation then is the beginning and the end of the development cycle. The only difference is that while at the beginning group members are objects of evangelisation, in the final stage they become the subjects – the evangelists themselves. "There is no place for passive members within our movement," Father Franciszek once said; "for those who seek merely their own enrichment. All who have discovered the light must take it to others." Indeed, within the last few years it has become the norm to test animators through their capacity to form a new evangelistic group and lead it through the whole development cycle. In this way the spiritual energy within the movement can be transformed into evangelistic dynamism and the movement continues to grow both in numbers and in spiritual maturity. The statistics so far support Father Blachnicki's reasoning. Within the last fifteen years the number of Oasis participants has increased more than twentyfold from a mere 3500 in 125 groups in the summer of 1972 to over 70,000 in 1986. It is not surprising that to ensure uniform formation within the collection of small groups an extensive selection of printed aids has been prepared and published, entirely without the censor's knowledge or approval. Every year each animator is given a folder containing several printed aids. Some are used during the retreat itself, others help the animator to lead the group between retreats; there are even guidelines as to the conduct of relations with the local authorities.

The Oasis Movement's rapid numerical growth and the complexity of its programmes resulted in a sudden shortage of leaders by the end of the 1970s. More priests and nuns were urgently needed who could act as moderators, and more committed lay people who had matured within the movement were required to oversee the running of the movement's diaconate, such as the crusade for the liberation of Man, or the plan for national evangelisation.

Fortunately since the late 1970s more than 50% of all young men entering Polish seminaries every year have been long-standing Light-Life members. The majority of them have maintained close ties with the movement, participating in the summer Oasis during their seven years at the seminary. They have become a fertile ground for the recruitment of new moderators. It was thanks to this group that so many Polish parishes were infected with enthusiasm for the movement and its vision of the local Church. Indeed in recent years some 1000 Polish priests have chosen to become members of a special priestly community within the Light-Life movement – the Community of Christ and Servant. The impact of this group on the Polish Church and also on Polish society as a whole cannot be overstated.

Since 1960 there has also been a permanent diaconate

for women – a group who have decided to dedicate their entire lives to promoting the Light-Life movement. The women's group is organised on a basis similar to the Evangelical Council of the first Christians. The young women make temporary vows at first, and then at the age of 30, permanent vows. Father Blachnicki supervised their spiritual development. They have remained the most dedicated and faithful of all of his helpers.

At the beginning when the movement was small in numbers and simple in its programme, it could be run almost entirely from the national centre at Krościenko by Father Franciszek and a handful of helpers. Later when its numbers reached tens of thousands scattered throughout Poland, a detailed structure was introduced which operates to this day. At the top of the pyramid is the national moderator, at a lower level – diocesan moderators. Within a parish several basic groups are each run by animators. To assist intellectual feedback and the "circulation" of spiritual life, community days are regularly organised at each level. Despite this hierarchical structure, there is no place in the movement for autocratic individuals. Every moderator, whether at parish or national level, is surrounded by a group of mainly lay helpers representing all existing diaconates. This group, together with the moderator, represents the smallest cell of a "diaconate of unity". The group meets together to pray, to study the Bible and to discuss the problems of the movement in the region. This diaconate of unity exists at all levels: parish, regional, diocesan and national. Father Franciszek's hope is that every Polish parish will be transformed into a true Christian Community based on Agape, so that in the end the whole of Poland would become one community living in Christ.

Then of course, the movement would become redun-
dant – at least in its present form. "What a paradox,"
someone once pointed out to Father Franciszek, "to
have self-annihilation as one's ultimate goal." "I would
rather call it self-fulfilment," replied Father Franciszek.

6

Towards a Polish Theology
of Liberation

On 16 October 1978 Cardinal Wojtyła, a long-standing
friend and staunch supporter of the Light-Life movement, was elected Pope John Paul II. Father Franciszek
planned a trip to Rome; he wanted to be present at the
Pope's enthronement. At first the authorities refused
him a passport but after the Secretary of the Polish
Episcopate intervened, they revoked their decision –
Father Franciszek was free to go. He wished he could
talk personally to the Pope, but thought this was unre-
alistic. After all there was a difference between Kraków,
where Cardinal Wojtyła was accessible at almost any
time, and Rome where he had to get past the almost
impenetrable Curia. Not quite knowing what to do he
decided to attend the Pope's first Wednesday general
audience in St Peter's Basilica. He chose a place near the
door. "Maybe there will be an opportunity to say a few
words to the Pope's Polish chaplain Dziwisz," thought
Father Franciszek, as he knew Father Dziwisz well from

his time in Kraków. After the audience the Pope was moving slowly towards the entrance door, when someone behind Father Franciszek shouted in Polish, "Blessed be Jesus Christ." The Pope stopped and looked in the direction of the cry. He immediately spotted Father Franciszek. "Professor," the Pope used his favourite phrase to describe Father Franciszek, "why don't you want to pay me a visit? Please come to supper tonight." At the table the Pope turned to Father Franciszek, "and what about Oasis? Does this mean that there will be no Oasis for me this summer?" After a while he said resolutely, "I know, come to Castel Gandolfo, put up your tents there and have an Oasis retreat." Father Franciszek accepted the invitation immediately and thus an Oasis of the third level, a "Roman Oasis", "Ecclesia Mater-Mater Ecclesia" was born.

In his farewell message to the Poles, the Pope made a special appeal to them to renew and uphold Christian values in Polish society: "I ask you to oppose all that degrades human dignity and demoralises a healthy society, that jeopardises its very existence and the common good, that diminishes its contribution to the common achievements of Humanity, of Christian nations and Christ's Church."

Father Franciszek's own picture of Poland in 1978 was far from rosy. According to official statistics the Poland of 1978 was the most alcoholic country in the world. The average Pole drank 8.9 litres of pure alcohol that year and there were 45,000 shops selling alcohol – one for every 750 people. Some 150 million zlotys were spent on alcohol, 1.5 million people were terminal alcoholics and over 5 million people drank to excess – which meant that they were drunk on average 240 times a year. Father Franciszek was particularly worried that the consumption of alcohol seemed to have increased continuously from 3.81 litres in 1960 to 8.9 litres of pure alcohol for every citizen in 1978. If the trend was not stopped, argued Father Franciszek, by 1990 the average consumption of alcohol would have increased to 17 litres with some 20 million people drinking excessively, 10-12 million drunk every day and four million terminal alcoholics. It was clear that the moral, psychological and biological consequences for the whole nation would be catastrophic.

Father Franciszek realised that it would be possible to use the unique authority of the first Polish Pope to mobilise Polish society in a national campaign against alcoholism. However, he did not want to use the Pope's authority in a superficially patriotic sense favoured by those who argued that Poland should try to live up to the expectations of the rest of the world as the country which had produced the first Slav Pope. Instead, Father Franciszek wanted to share with the people the Pope's teaching and his vision of twentieth-century man, man entangled in all the complexities of the Polish situation.

Five days after the Pope's appeal to the Poles to uphold Christian values, Father Blachnicki went on Vatican Radio and broadcast a message to all members of the Light-Life movement announcing his idea of a "Crusade for the Liberation of Man" from all social plagues, especially from alcohol. The Crusade was to be officially proclaimed during the Pope's first home-coming, planned for the summer of 1979.

Father Franciszek returned to Krościenko and a hectic period of planning for the Crusade began. It involved meetings with anti-alcohol experts, several retreats for possible future leaders of the Crusade, discussions of the theological foundations of the Crusade at the fourth annual congress of Light-Life leaders and a pilot parish retreat with the "Gospel of Liberation" as the main theme. By May 1979 a programme for the Crusade had been drawn up and 100 people joined it, pledging total abstinence from alcohol. Father Franciszek saw the Crusade as a continuation of his anti-alcoholic campaign of the 1950's. The proclamation of the Crusade did not alter the identity and programme of the Light-Life movement. "The Crusade", explained Father Franciszek, "should be regarded as the movement's Christian service to Poland." Thus he expected that all members of the movement would join in the Crusade by giving individual pledges. However, the Crusade's main targets were all people of goodwill who were ready to give up alcohol voluntarily in order to set an example to others. Thus membership of the Crusade was to exceed, by far, that of the Light-Life movement.

A special "Diaconate of Liberation" within the Light-Life movement was to be created at national, regional and local levels to give an impetus to the Crusade and to prepare materials and visual aids needed for the campaign. News of the Crusade began to spread and by the time the Pope arrived in Warsaw several hundred people had already signed a pledge of total alcohol abstinence in a "Liberation Book" which was to be blessed by the Pope. All along Father Franciszek had hoped that in his overcrowded itinerary John Paul II would find time for a meeting with Oasis friends. The only problem seemed to be where and when such an encounter should take place. When he heard that the Pope was to celebrate a Mass for the highlanders of Nowy Targ, situated a mere

30 km from Krościenko, Father Franciszek suggested
with his usual boldness that the Light-Life movement
should invite the Pope to its Krościenko centre as it was
"on the way, anyway". The idea caught on immediately
and in mid-April 1979 John Paul II was handed a letter
inviting him to Krościenko. "In recent years," the letter
said, "Krościenko has become for many Poles a symbol
of the freedom of the spirit, of the victory of faith . . .
and therefore the 'Crusade for the Liberation of Man',
which pursues its mission under the banner 'Have no
fear', could be proclaimed and blessed in this place,
which would have an enormous symbolic significance
– historically as well as morally."

Many, including Father Franciszek, were worried that
Kopia Górka was not prepared to take the several thousand guests expected if the Pope came to Krościenko.
"What about building permission?" asked a close friend
of Father Franciszek's. "It would take months, if not
years." Father Franciszek refused to be defeated. "There
is no time to lose," he argued, "we know that building
permission will not be granted anyway." Soon the construction of an amphitheatre on Kopia Górka was under
way. It was to have 3000 seats. In addition there were
paths to be built, as well as a sewage purification plant
and many other smaller jobs – all to be done within a
month.

One day a government commission descended on
Krościenko and sealed off the whole building site.
Father Blachnicki, always calm during moments of
greatest tension, asked that the seals should be removed
and the work continued. A few days later the commission reappeared, this time backed by a lorry load of
militiamen, and sealed everything again. Threats were

made that there would be the gravest consequences if the seals were broken again. Someone phoned Father Franciszek who was away in Zakopane. His reaction was typical: "That is a pity. We will have to break the seals again." So they did and finished all the work uninterrupted. In the last two weeks of May several dozen bricklayers, carpenters, plumbers, electricians, welders and decorators, inspired by the hope of a visit from John Paul II, were working in two shifts from 5 a.m. until midnight.

On Friday 1 June – the eve of the Pope's arrival in Poland – some 200 people were already in Krościenko. By Saturday the number swelled to 400. The annual central Oasis began its summer programme, interrupted by transmissions of the Pope's visit on TV and radio, watched by everyone. Everyone was anxiously waiting for the Pope's response. "Will he or won't he?" was the question on everyone's minds; the usual answer being "God only knows". Then Father Franciszek received news that the Pope could not come to Krościenko. A delegation from the Oasis Movement was welcome to join in the Pope's Mass in Nowy Targ, he was told, but any special meeting between Oasis and the Pope before or after the Mass was impossible. However, the Liberation Book signed by the Pope beforehand could be presented to Father Franciszek during the Mass and the Crusade's pledge recited publicly at the end. It was also agreed that the Pope would hand over to the movement twelve baskets full of Bibles, which he had brought with him from Rome and that he would bless the foundation stone of a church which was to be built with money people had donated instead of buying alcohol.

Father Franciszek welcomed the new arrangement as a visible sign of God's providence. "Now the proclamation of the Crusade will be heard and seen by hundreds of thousands of people present at Mass and on television. Could there be a better launch for our Crusade?"

On Thursday evening, 7 June 1979, the new amphitheatre in Krościenko – named after John Paul II – was full to capacity for the first time. A gathering of some 2000 people was preparing for a 30 kilometre night-walk to Nowy Targ. For the young pilgrims it was a night to remember. In almost every house they passed on the way, a large portrait of the Polish Pope was displayed, surrounded and lit up by small electric bulbs. At junctions crowds of people waited to join the marches. No one minded an hour-long storm; the torrential rain was accepted as a special "Christening". Nevertheless when the group arrived in Nowy Targ in the small hours of Friday morning they were truly grateful for the countless cups of tea offered by the local people. The last two kilometres took several hours to negotiate but at last the whole Oasis group filled the sector right in front of the podium where the Papal Mass was to be celebrated. Now they only had to wait for their first sight of the Papal helicopter. It arrived promptly at 10.15 a.m.

At the end of his sermon, but before the Credo, someone in the Oasis sector struck up the Pope's favourite "Oasis" song, which they had sung together at the end of the last meeting in Kluszkowice. The Pope stood motionless. When the singing stopped, he said, "I want to remind you, when we sang this song the last time." Here, his voice suddenly broke. After a pause he continued, with tears in his eyes: "It was on a small hill in Kluszkowice at the beginning of June. I hope you will sing this song again for me in Rome."

The Mass continued. A delegation from Light-Life led the offertory procession. They handed the Pope the Liberation Book and all the members of the movement present repeated after Father Blachnicki, "Immaculate Mother of the Church: we look to you as the example of a person saved and liberated, and through love absolutely devoted to Christ in the Spirit. We are aware of all kinds of slavery in which our hearts are entangled and from which we wish to liberate ourselves. We stretch out our hands towards our brothers who as yet have not experienced the freedom of the sons of God, we commend ourselves to you, so that by the power of the same spirit which acted in you, we might give ourselves up to Christ and through Him to the Father. To your hands we commend our pledge to abstain from alcohol, so that by becoming truly independent from it, we might set free those brothers who cannot do it on their own. Through this act of love we wish to serve our brothers just like Christ, who out of love for us, humbled himself and became a servant. We commend to you the entire Crusade for the Liberation of Man, and wish that it may become a tool in your hand for the Liberation of our nation." The Crusade for the Liberation of Man was then proclaimed.

By the end of 1980 some 7000 people had signed the pledge in the liberation book kept in Krościenko. However, Father Franciszek had already realised that if the Crusade was to be successful on a national scale, it had to be preceded by evangelisation. For only through awakening in man, faith in Christ, can the power of the Gospel reveal itself by rescuing a human being from enslavement and transforming him into a free man. In March 1980 at the fifth annual congress of Light-Life leaders, at the most famous Polish Marian shrine of Jasna Góra, Father Franciszek put forward a new plan of evangelisation – Ad Christum Redemptorem – on a national scale, which was to be combined with the Crusade for the Liberation of Man. The plan was inspired by Pope Paul VI's exhortation *Evangelii Muntiandi*, and Pope John Paul II's encyclical *Redemptor Hominis* but it was also strongly influenced by the emerging emphasis of John Paul II's pontificate – the inextricable bond between evangelisation and the liberation of man. In Father Blachnicki's plans, National Evangelisation was to begin with prayer.

"Whosoever undertakes evangelisation," he declared, "soon realises that this work surpasses the capabilities of man. For this is the work of God, performed by God through the Son and the Holy Spirit. Man is called to participate in this mission, but he should be aware of his own limitations and base his trust in its success on the power of God. That is why we are beginning our National Evangelisation with intensive prayer. During his visit to Poland, John Paul II ended his first sermon with a prophetic call: 'May Your Spirit descend! May Your Spirit descend and change the face of the land – this land!' In that prayer the Holy Father summarised the goal of his pilgrimage as well as the desire of his heart. In it he also revealed that he was not counting on himself but had put his trust in the power of the Holy Spirit. Following the Pope's thoughts, we should try to understand the realities of Poland in 1980 – whilst being careful not to escape into history. Poles so readily identify themselves with history and like to talk of Poland being faithful to Christ for the last thousand years while forgetting the sad picture of contemporary Poland. This 'always faithful' Poland is in danger and the danger stems from our unfaithfulness to the Gospel. 1.5 million unborn children killed in their mother's womb is a reality of Poland in 1980. Ten litres of alcohol drunk annually by every Pole: this is the reality of our land. The reality of 1980 is that 50% of Poles are practising non-believers, who come to the church once or twice a year while leading a pagan life. Reality in 1980 means the millions of people who have renounced Christ and are used as unresisting tools by those who plan to destroy not only the Church but also all human values. Millions of baptised Polish Catholics are unresisting tools of our system.

This means that we ourselves, with our own hands, are destroying our country while simultaneously reciting slogans about our Christian history. We participate in pilgrimages, celebrate anniversaries, readily identifying ourselves with past generations and feel good in that Poland of the Saints. My criticism does not mean that we should not learn from history. However, this should be incorporated into our own lives and our values. Therefore, first and foremost, we should pluck up our courage so that when we pray for the Holy Spirit to renew this land, we should see it for what it really is. Perhaps we should take the most recent yearbook of our region and pray for all the thousands of people living there. We should have at the forefront of our minds all those who are members of the local Communist party and who are working for a plan which is not God's plan of salvation but the plan of Satan; all those who work for the Security Police, belong to an atheist association or propagate abortion. Then suddenly we shall realise that in our proverbially Catholic country, there are so many people who need to discover Christ, and need our help. There is also an urgent need to change our attitude to prayer. Intellectually we accept that all men have been redeemed by Christ and believe that every man is called to salvation and can be converted as long as he lives. Moreover, often, when someone wants to pray for say . . . the first secretary of the Party or the local head of the Security Police, we find it strange. Some break into laughter even though such prayers should be seen as the natural consequence of our Christian faith. Modern man should pray with the Bible in one hand and a yearbook in the other. Only then will it be a true prayer for the renewal of our land."

According to Father Blachnicki's plan, Oases for Prayer were to be set up in every one of the 49 administrative districts of Poland. The groups were to meet once a month for prayer, thus taking responsibility for their part of the Polish land. Oasis for Prayer was in due course to produce people who would join in a "diaconate of evangelisation" and reach every Pole with the Good News through individual contacts but mainly through an evangelistic parish retreat. An elaborate programme for such a retreat was worked out. All members of an evangelistic group were to try and visit everyone living within the boundaries of the parish and personally invite them to come and participate in the retreat. At its centre was a film version of the Gospel of St Luke – a gift from Western Protestants. An important part of the retreat consisted of testimonies given by people who had already discovered Christ. Everyone present was also given a copy of St Luke's Gospel and invited to come to a series of "meetings with St Luke's Gospel". The aim of these meetings was to introduce the participants to the Crusade and lead them to make a pledge of abstinence.

Ad Christum Redemptorem was welcomed enthusiastically by the 460 local leaders of the Light-Life movement gathered at the shrine of Jasna Góra. However, there were other difficult issues to be discussed.

In the aftermath of the workers' strike of 1976 and the repressions that followed, a small committee of intellectuals, KOR, was set up to defend the workers: it aimed to collect money for their families, to provide the accused with legal aid and to publicise their plight. Soon it began to circulate a bulletin informing the public of developments. Since 1976 a powerful dissident movement had grown up despite police harrassment. It concentrated on clandestine publishing, on organising discussion groups and even public demonstrations. The many unofficial periodicals which now began to appear revealed the enormous damage inflicted on Polish economic and cultural life by 30 years of misleading propaganda. Irrespective of their political preferences, all the opposition groups agreed that the process of social disintegration had to be resisted through moral revival; people needed to find the courage to be themselves and to reject a life based on hypocrisy and fear, the two pillars of a Communist totalitarian state. By fighting for national moral revival, the dissidents found that they were defending the same values as those upheld by the Church, which they had come to regard as the chief moral authority in Poland. They supported the Church's struggle for believers' rights. The unofficial press reported every major event in the Church's life and published the uncensored texts of sermons and pastoral letters. By 1980 it had become obvious that Catholics formed a large part of the dissident movement and regarded the Church as a natural ally. Father Blachnicki felt strongly that the issue of current political dissent should not be avoided especially with regard to the coming elections and the dissidents' appeals to boycott them. Young people, he argued, had a right to expect clear moral guidance from the Church in every sphere of life including that of political involvement.

One result of a lengthy discussion by the 460 delegates was a declaration, which was to become widely known, concerning the involvement of members of the movement in the campaign to overcome the nation's problems. It showed that the Light-Life movement's aim in organising retreats or other activities for spiritual renewal was not to enable Christians to escape from the problems of Polish life, but to equip them to make a distinctively Christian contribution to solving these problems.

"Poland is unusual," the declaration states, "in that all its moral and religious crises can be largely attributed to a single cause – the present political situation, both internal and external. The question therefore arises as to whether activities aimed at liberating either individuals or the nation as a whole from all manner of evil will have to assume a political character. Certainly, from the 'other side's' point of view, any activity which is effective, i.e. which leads to real changes in the existing situation, will be considered political. But how will Christians view such activity?

"The documents of the Second Vatican Council clearly define the principles by which Catholics should be guided in their political activities. Indeed, such activities, on the understanding that they are directed towards the common good, are approved of and are even, to a certain extent, considered to be the duty of all Christians.

"However, it is impossible for people who live under a totalitarian regime to engage in legal political activity without being manipulated by the prevailing political forces in a manner contrary to their Christian conscience and the Church's directives. This is why Christians in Poland tend to deride the very idea of 'political involve-ment' and have on the whole resigned themselves to avoiding all political activity. Is there not a danger, however, that as a result of this we will abdicate our responsibilities and withdraw into 'oases' for the elite? Christians have found one way which, though not 'political' in the true sense of the word, does have the power to liberate individuals and even a whole nation. It is the way of Jesus Christ, of which John Paul II reminded us in his encyclical *Redemptor Hominis*: 'Jesus Christ meets the man of every age, including our own, with the same words: "You will know the truth, and the truth will make you free" ' (John 8: 32). These words contain both a fundamental requirement and a warning: the requirement of an honest relationship with truth as a condition for authentic freedom, and the warning to avoid every kind of illusory freedom that fails to enter into the whole truth about man and the world. Today also, even after two thousand years, we see Christ as the one who brings man freedom based on truth.

"It is the fact that we are forced to live in a perma-nent state of hypocrisy that is the real source, even the essence, of our captivity. The man who lives in harmony with himself, with his conscience, with his calling and, ultimately, with the divine concept of himself as a free spirit, is truly free. Even though he be in chains, behind prison bars, or surrounded by the barbed wire of a labour camp the promise that 'the truth will make you free' is fulfilled. This way of freedom – through bearing witness to the truth – is open to everyone, but to reach it we must first break down the one barrier which prevents us from bearing witness, the barrier of fear.

"On a more practical level, we would like to stress one or two instances in which a Christian is urgently required to bear witness to the truth. First let us take the forthcoming 'election'. In fact, what we have is not an election, but a heavily weighted referendum, in which we are expected to express our support for a totalitarian, one-party system of government and to vote for anonymous candidates in whose selection we have no say whatsoever. In this situation, taking part in an election is for a Christian not so much a political act as a matter of conscience. Those who can say in all sincerity that they have confidence in the present system of government and in its programme, aims and methods, should assert this publicly by taking part in the election. Those, on the other hand, whose conscience does not allow them to express such confidence in the government should abstain from taking part in the election since this is the only possible way for people in their situation to witness to the truth.

"In the same way, those who consider themselves Christians, but who also belong to the Communist

Party or to some other association with a similar ideological basis and similar aims, should reconsider their position. We cannot ignore the clear and unequivocal words of Christ: 'No man can serve two masters.'

"Another question which must be raised concerns our attitude towards those brave people who, at great risk to themselves, undertake in various ways, but without using violence or force, to fight for justice, freedom and basic human rights in our society. We would like to suggest that by their courageous witness to the truth and defence of basic human rights, sometimes at the risk of their lives, these people have earned our deepest admiration, moral support and any further help we can give them within the dictates of Christian love and wisdom. Finally we would like to express our conviction that Catholics and other Christians in Poland are now in an exceptionally advantageous position, in that the present situation affords many opportunities to bear witness to Christ and His truth. The Church in Poland will suffer irreparable damage if we fail to respond to God's call to bear witness to the truth in our everyday lives.

"Since we are a renewal movement with 'Light-Life' as our motto, we feel a special responsibility to reflect in our lives the light of truth which we perceive through faith, and to eliminate all contradiction between the faith we profess and the way we live. We want to do so in a spirit of Christian love towards all men, in particular those enslaved by false doctrines and those who, although they know the truth, are not courageous enough to follow Christ and allow the truth to set them free."

All 460 delegates signed the declaration. By the

time the leaders met again at the end of August in Krościenko to assess the summer Oasis retreats, in the Gdańsk shipyard an inter-factory strike committee "Solidarity" was finalising its historic agreement with Party representatives – signed on 31st August. The free trade union Solidarity was born and with it, as was then believed, a new Poland.

In accordance with the Jasna Góra declaration, the Light-Life movement did not want to remain outside the current events but accepted them as a challenge to which it should respond. This response came in the form of a "recommendation" to all members of the Light-Life movement, passed by the Sixth National Congress of the movement's leaders. After readopting the programme of liberation through truth and love, the movement officially declared that, as part of the world-wide "non-violence" movement, it would undertake a campaign to liberate people from any form of enslavement in the manner revealed by Christ in His Gospel.

"We discovered the ultimate source of the unity which we wish to serve," the leaders stated. "This is the compassion of God, to which we turn in the third eucharistic prayer with the words:

'In your mercy, O Father, unite your children scattered throughout the world.'

This discovery we regard as the main fruit of the Sixth National Congress.

"We also turned to John Paul II's encyclical on God's mercy, *Dives in Misericordia*. Against the background of the general situation of threat and fear described in the Pope's encyclical, we want to analyse our own

Polish form of this menace. At the time of our Congress, tensions seem to be relaxing and the political and social situation is quietening down. Nevertheless, unease remains. Everyone recognises the temporary nature of the understandings reached. True, there have been plenty of declarations of wonderful programmes, optimistic assurances and calls to reform. The question is, what intentions do these declarations conceal? Do those who make them really want what they assert or can they not frame their words differently at present? It is disturbing that we search in advance for a code to decipher the message concealed in every declaration. We look for the true intention which the spoken words do not reveal but which is veiled with all the skill of rhetoric. It is particularly sad that even avowed Catholics at times use 'diplomatic' speech unhesitatingly, afraid to call a spade a spade.

"Of those who hold power, few convince us that their words are not just another form of political propaganda, that they have any intention other than defending their authority.

"Those who declare themselves for liberty are also faced with the dilemma of truth: between truth to the bitter end, and truth which it is proper to reveal at a given moment - 'tactical' or limited truth.

"In short, the situation shows no prospect of an ultimate solution but bears the hallmarks of improvisation, which in itself is a source of anxiety or fear, a fear shared by all who have not yet discovered the way to true freedom.

"Anxiety and fear describe not only our internal situation but also our relations with neighbouring countries. We are afraid about 'what may be inflicted upon others by military means'. Those who hold powerful means of pressure in their hands cannot stop worrying over what will happen to them when others cease to fear these means.

"Our country and the world need nothing more today than people who have attained total freedom. Only those who are freed in this way can bring liberty to others; people set free by truth because they had the courage to admit it and act accordingly. Only then does Our Lord's promise become fulfilled: 'No follower of mine shall wander in the dark; he shall have the light of life' (John 8: 12). Our country and the world need teachers of the truth, not formal teachers but those who witness by the purity of their intentions, disinterestedly and devotedly yielding their lives to the truth, and if necessary, sacrificing them for it. The Polish form of menace and anxiety at the present time consists of a manifestation of the general crisis over truth in human relationships, lack of responsibility toward the truth, a purely materialistic relationship to fellow men, and loss of a sense of the common good, all of which the Pope speaks of in his encyclical. In such a situation we must look to the words of Christ. 'The truth will set you free' (John 8: 32). For if, in the spirit of Christ's words, truth liberates man, then it follows that his enslavement depends on falsehood. Belief in the basic lie suggested to man by the tempter: 'You will become like gods'; that is, a lie concerning metaphysical self-awareness, is the origin of man's state of serfdom. The man who gives way to lies and reliance on falsehood is the most pitiable and the most deserving of help. To confirm him in this falsehood, leaving him with his delusions actually injures him, whereas freeing him from falsehood is a true and basic work of mercy – on the condition, of course, that the motive is not a desire to shame him or humiliate him. The motive should be love and the desire to free him from evil.

"In imitating God, the Father of mercy whose countenance was revealed to us by Christ in the parable of the prodigal son, the man wishing to free another through the truth concentrates particularly on the dignity of man, wishing to save that dignity and human nature itself (*Dives in Misericordia* 32). To preserve human dignity is voluntarily to surrender one's will and give up one's life to the imparted truth: 'let us speak the truth in love' (Eph. 4: 15). Such true love is described in the New Testament as Agape.

"In this manner we are to undertake a diaconate of liberty through truth in our country. Unless that mission were linked to love and mercy it would be threatened by distortion through pride, contamination through hatred and a triumphalism founded on a desire for victory and the downfall of the other side, rather than the desire to save or help the other. Only by associating the two missions – liberation through the truth and liberation through love – can we call ourselves the disciples of Christ. We consciously associate ourselves with the great, world-wide movement of 'non-violence' which campaigns to liberate people from all forms of enslavement and violence, in the manner revealed by Christ in the Gospels. This path renounces the use of force but aims to reinstate justice and freedom by liberating those who forcibly perpetrate injustice and violence.

"We are confronted by the splendid revolution of the workers, signified by the word 'Solidarity' which has shaken the country and the whole world. It was launched, not in the name of materialism, but in order to rescue man, whom the system had overlooked. We stand before this reality with amazement, gratitude and a new hope.

"However, we are uneasy about its future and further development, being aware of the dangers which threaten it from within and without as a result of human weakness and imperfection. The question arises: what can we, what should be do as members of the Light–Life movement? The following positive replies come to mind:

(a) We must respond through the diaconate of prayer, first of all prayer for God's mercy and for His intercession for our country and the world today. We wish to ask for help from the Holy Spirit for those who are struggling for truth and justice, that they may continue. We must pray for those who especially need mercy, who are still slaves to falsehood.

(b) Faced with the conditions in Poland, our response must be a diaconate of evangelisation. In the conviction that only Jesus Christ is the ultimate guarantor of freedom and respect for the dignity of man, we wish to introduce Him to all those who do not yet know Him, who have not received Him personally into their lives as their one and only Lord and Saviour. We wish to be included in the great evangelistic work of Ad Christum Redemptorem. We wish to reach the greatest possible number of people in our homeland, especially those in places of work, and workers associated with Solidarity. By organising evangelistic retreats for them we hope to help them discover the foundation and sources of true Solidarity in Christ.

(c) Our next response will be a diaconate of mercy. We realise that evangelisation, declaring God's mercy, cannot be credible or fruitful without demonstrating that mercy to our brethren, and especially to the suffering, the hungry and the persecuted. In our movement we wish to start a 'diaconate of mercy' to help with those charitable works which the Church must carry out now in Poland for the sake of the hungry, the sick and the lonely, large families, the families of alcoholics, etc.

(d) Finally there must be a greater involvement in a diaconate of liberation, especially in the crusade for the liberation of man. In this field, three definite tasks stand out as the most urgent.

– Liberation by testifying to the truth in a spirit of love and in a spirit of non-violence.

– Liberation from alcoholism (the most common form of subjection) which renders man incapable of preserving his dignity and self-respect.

– Liberation from the most developed form of egoism, dependence upon abortion. This form of bondage, arising from man's treating another human being as the subject for exploitation (so common among us) represents a biological threat to the nation's existence.

"All these tasks should become our diaconate among the Polish people as we search for the attainment of true freedom."

In December 1980 the parish priest of Our Lady of Perpetual Succour in Gdynia invited the Light-Life movement to organise a week-long parish evangelistic retreat. It fell on the tenth anniversary of the massacre of shipyard workers who were shot while returning to work in answer to the authorities' appeals. Among those who came to the retreat were many who had witnessed the tragic events of the 1970s; many who had lost their relatives and friends. In an atmosphere full of memories it was only natural that the concept of the Cross became central to all discussions. The theme of the Cross also predominated during the spontaneous testimonies given by some present in the church. One such testimony, by a member of the Gdańsk shipyard management team, gave a unique view of the famous strikes on the Polish Baltic coast in August 1980 which gave rise to the trade union Solidarity. "I should like to recall the words of Christ which have been repeated so often during this retreat, 'I am the Way, the Truth and the Light', and to remember December 1970. So many innocent people died. There was a change at the top. The new Party bosses promised us much – in return they demanded better productivity. People believed the new leaders and their promises . . . then they lost their trust in them and revolted again in 1976. Those who went on strike were later persecuted, arrested and intimidated. People waited in hope of a change until they could wait no more and in 1980 an 'explosion' occurred. Poles stood up to fight for social justice, to defend human dignity. It was at this time that crosses were erected on our plants. Solidarity with Christ, who died for our salvation on the cross, was growing . . . and it was to Him that the striking Poles turned for help. Masses were said at our plant. This was something incredible. It was through this Cross, through solidarity with Christ and his mother that we persevered."

Soon after this retreat Father Blachnicki formulated his "Polish Theology of Liberation" through truth.

"The Polish theology of liberation can be understood

fully only against the background of the spiritual state of the world, or rather the attitude of believers in the world. One may identify three typical concepts existing at present. The first two are in fact misconceptions which constantly reappear in history in attempts to create communities of faith. The third corresponds to a concept of faith based on the Bible, especially the New Testament.

"In the first concept, faith is understood as an escape into the hereafter. The faithful withdraw 'into inwardness of spiritual bliss' and leave the things of this world to float. The inner personal relationship with Jesus, the Redeemer, is considered the essential element of Christianity, which fills one with joy so great that the problems of this world are forgotten, as if in Jesus one had already discovered heaven on earth. This is a sentimental attitude to faith which alienates people from the realities of this world, which are dismissed as politics, or as the 'preoccupations of the children of this world'.

"This is characteristic, for example, of the Jesus movement, which developed out of the hippy phenomenon. It is also true of some groups within the charismatic movement (especially those in the initial stages of their development), as well as various movements within the free churches. All these phenomena could be described as 'Jesus movements'. This kind of separation between faith and participation in the events of this world can also occur if the faith is superficial and weak and not built upon a personal relationship with Christ in the Holy Spirit, but rather upon habit or religious upbringing.

"It results in a certain schizophrenia between an isolated religious sphere of conscience and the rest of life,

113

which develops according to its own standards and has nothing to do with faith. Unfortunately, this is the way that a great many practising Catholics understand their faith. In the long term such an attitude usually leads to unbelief.

"The second concept views faith as an external, supplementary motivation for social or political activity which represents one's primary goal. According to this concept, Christianity and even the Church are supposed to be merely useful supporters for a social revolution in the struggle for liberation. This applies above all to those movements in South America which may be grouped under the banner of the 'theology of liberation', although there are also less radical movements whose social, economic and political activities are carried out in the name of Christianity. The representatives of such movements should ask themselves to what extent their Christian involvement is based on a spiritual foundation and is open to the working of God's Spirit. If the first concept of faith may be described as 'Jesus movements', the second could be called 'Christ movements'. It is not the person of Jesus and a personal relationship with Him through faith which are paramount here, but rather His messianic deeds, which are expressed by his name Christ – the Anointed One.

"In reality, Jesus is the Christ and thus He must be present in our concept of faith. Jesus, the Son of the Living God, calls us and enables us through the gift of His Spirit to encounter Him personally, and later to be united with Him. At the same time, He invites us to share in His mission. As Christians, we are anointed together with Him, the Anointed One, and thereby called to participate in the redemption of the world in our given time and situation. Therefore we cannot consider our faith to be an escape into a blissful Me-You relationship with Jesus, but rather as a demand to participate with Christ, God's servant, in service for our brothers, so that through our responsible love and willingness to sacrifice they might be led to redemption and liberation in the power of Christ's cross. A personal relationship with God through Christ in the Holy Spirit is naturally the everlasting source of power, courage and enthusiasm for this service of liberation.

"This is the way that faith is understood in the Bible: as a call to a Me-You relationship with God but also as an anointing for service in fulfilling God's plan of redemption in the here and now of history. Faith, in other words, must be understood as participation in the self-consciousness of Jesus Christ, which he revealed in the synagogue at Nazareth at the beginning of his messianic activity with the words: 'The spirit of the Lord has been given to me, for He has anointed me. He has sent me to bring the good news to the poor, to proclaim liberty to captives and to the blind new sight, to set the down-trodden free, to proclaim the Lord's year of favour!' (Luke 4: 13-19).

"A blind man cannot be free – he has to be led by someone: a man who recovers his sight – who discovers the truth, becomes a free man. These two are inextricably bound together. It is when the truth as recognised by the intellect – the Light – is in harmony with one's behaviour – the Life – that the essential truth is victorious in us. At the same time this is also a formula for our liberation.

"When there is a discrepancy between Light and Life we become slaves. Today many of us are slaves in our own country. We all know the truth but do not speak it out because we know the consequences. If we speak we all too often simply report lies. Even when we know that something is white we say that it is black for we have been told to see it as black. Our whole life becomes a lie and there lies the essence of our humiliation, the loss of our dignity. A group of men overcome by evil, hatred and the desire for power, which should be God's alone, look down on us rejoicing to see all these people venerating them idolatrously by repeating what they are told to say.

"To abide and persist in truth means to bear witness to the truth in one's life and to live according to the truth. To do so one must overcome the fear which keeps us from speaking and living the truth. We have to realise that only when we have the courage to bear witness to the truth, regardless of the consequences, will we become free men. For enslavement is caused not so much by outside factors such as violence but by fear. If the majority of Poles plucked up their courage to live by the truth and to unmask lies we would already be a free society: our enemies would be helpless. They are powerful only if they can intimidate us into pretending that we believe in their lies, when we ourselves repeat them against our will and our beliefs. This situation cannot prevail forever, for man has been created to be free. It was this yearning for freedom which was at the core of the postwar revolts in Poland in 1956, 1968, 1970, 1976 and most notably in 1980.

"A person finds the courage to bear witness to the truth when he is willing to make sacrifices for the truth, to the point of sacrificing one's life as Christ did. The mystery of the Cross is the key element of this Polish

Theology of Liberation. In fact without it no Theology of Liberation can be constructed.

"The question arises. How does one come by the readiness to suffer, to take up the cross? This leads to the still missing element of the theology of liberation. This element is trust in God, faith in the love of God who receives and rewards our readiness to sacrifice, springing from the love and trust of a child and through a new life in the resurrection. This trust in God in the hour of our death is also the attitude of Christ on the cross. Everyone must adopt this attitude in order to achieve inner freedom: in other words, they participate in Christ's Son-Father relationship.

"Similarly, the New Testament expresses the problem of human freedom through the idea of being children of God: 'For all who are led by the Spirit of God are sons of God. For you did not receive the spirit of slavery to fall back into fear, but you have received the spirit of sonship. When we cry, "Abba, Father" it is the Spirit himself bearing witness with our spirit that we are children of God' (Rom. 8: 14-16). Likewise we read in Galatians: 'So with us; when we were children, we were slaves to the elemental spirit of the universe. But when the time had fully come, God sent forth his Son, born of woman, born under the law, so that we might receive adoption as sons. And because you are sons God has sent the Spirit of his Son into our heart, crying "Abba, Father!" So through God you are no longer a slave but a son, and if a son then an heir' (Gal. 4: 3-7). One can see in these texts that the scriptures do not know the alternative: Slave – Lord; but rather the alternative Son – Father.

"It is not the person who makes others his slaves, who

117

is free. Rather it is the person, who as a son, freely places himself in the service of the Father out of love. A free person expresses himself by serving others, his brothers, as Christ did. Brotherhood is an integral element of this Theology of Liberation. People who have the same father are brothers. Accepting the fatherhood of God and becoming children of God through Christ and his Spirit, is the only way to true human brotherhood. Without this all talks about brotherhood remain empty slogans. Only where brotherhood in Christ is realised is there no room for manipulating people, for treating them as objects. It is in brotherhood expressed in the spirit of mutual service that the true freedom of society lies. This is the freedom of God's children, and it is for this freedom that Christ set us free."

Autumn 1981 was marked by increasing tension. Solidarity fought to consolidate the gains of August 1980, though by now there could be little doubt as to the real intentions of the Polish authorities. Many members of the movement were active members of Solidarity. Within the movement an initiative called the "Independent Christian–Social Service" was born, in order to promote the Movement's concept of liberation among members of Solidarity. In November 1981 the programme of the Christian Service "Truth–Liberation" was presented to a group of Solidarity activists in Lublin. It was later presented to Solidarity members in Kraków, Wrocław, Poznań, Gdańsk and Warsaw. Fifteen hundred copies of the bulletin *Truth and Liberation* were distributed. On 28 November 1981, during a sit-in strike at the Catholic University of Lublin, the first committee of the "Independent Christian Service – Truth and Liberation" was assembled. However, on 13 December martial law was declared upon the people of Poland. The Polish communists were re-establishing by force their absolute power over society. The "Independent Christian Service – Truth and Liberation", like all other initiatives not subordinated to the Party, was overnight officially branded as highly treasonable. Sixteen months of hope were dashed.

7

God's or Caesar's

The independent Catholic Light–Life movement, which operates openly, is directed from a national centre and is active throughout the country among all sections of society. It is a unique phenomenon in the Eastern bloc. It was created despite the fact that in the light of all state laws and official policy on religion it should never have existed. Everything that is essential to the movement was forbidden as illegal in Poland from the start. In a Communist system only the Party is allowed to organise and lead the forces which form society. This is especially true in relation to youth work. This axiom is safeguarded by a whole series of laws and regulations. Yet, one by one, the Light–Life movement broke all decrees restricting religion which had been observed by the Church for years: decrees on gatherings, on associations, on control of the press. "These decrees were broken not because the movement sought confrontation with the authorities," Father Franciszek explained, "but because we just wanted to live." The Life of the Church required believers to gather together to form communities and associations. "We never sought confrontation, although obviously, by its very existence the movement was destroying the model of the Church imposed on us by the atheist authorities – confined within the four walls of the sacristy, limited to worship alone." "In fact," he continued, "what Solidarity has achieved in the socio-political sphere, had developed within the Light-Life movement much earlier – the courage to question and reject the rigid forms of behaviour and thinking imposed by the Party. We always rejected any cautious diplomacy and followed the principle of never asking what we were allowed to do, but rather doing what we had to as Christians who wanted to live according to the Gospel in the freedom of God's children. We never let fear keep us from doing what we felt we must do as disciples of Christ. After all, there is only one danger a Christian should fear – that of losing his faith. Consequently year after year the movement grew, never taking a step back out of fear. Here lies the essence of our success."

Over the years many attempts were made by the Polish authorities to infiltrate the Light-Life movement, to restrict its activities and even to destroy it totally. In the sixties when the movement was still small in size and influence, petty harassment such as interrogation, blackmail and refusal to permit travel (even to other Communist bloc countries), was directed only at the most active members. In the 1970s when the movement had grown to number thousands, systematic repressions began, although by that time Oasis was already under the protection of the Polish hierarchy, being described officially as "a part of the Church's pastoral mission", and a special agreement on Oasis retreats had been signed by the Church and State authorities. At first, most of the bishops saw the movement as a vehicle for introducing the vernacular liturgy in the Catholic Church of Poland in accordance with the instruments of the Second Vatican Council. Only a few, among them Cardinal Wojtyła of Kraków realised the unique opportunity, which the movement offered, of influencing whole sections of society. In December 1976 Cardinal Wojtyła organised the official presentation of the Oasis movement before the Episcopal Commission for the Lay Apostolate, of which he was the head. With time, most of the bishops realised that in the face of the intensive de-Christianisation pursued ruthlessly by the atheist state, the Church should respond by Christianising just as intensely. With all the legal restrictions, new forms had to be found and suddenly the Light-Life movement appeared an ideal vehicle for the task.

Despite the protection of the Episcopate and the Church-State agreement, by the mid-1970s harassment of Father Blachnicki and his close associates had increased. The Oasis house on the Kopia mountain in Krościenko was heavily taxed and attempts were being made to instal bugging devices in it, as well as a "lodger" – an obvious informer. The movement's activists were continuously detained for questioning without warrants of arrest. The questions they were asked varied from inquiries concerning the private life of Father Blachnicki, to the meaning of the movement's badge. Secondary school leavers were told that they would not get a place at any university if they retained their links with the movement; students and young professionals were worried that they would be wrecking their future career prospects unless they broke with the movement immediately.

There were several attempts at crude provocation. One day a resident of the house on the Kopia mountain found pistol bullets in his wardrobe. Father Blachnicki was sure that there would be an imminent house search in which they would be found. The number of ways that such discoveries could be used was almost limitless – from discrediting Father Blachnicki's credibility as a spokesman for non-violence to a criminal charge of organising terrorism behind the smoke screen of a religious movement. For several hours all the people living in the house searched for a gun, fearing it was also hidden somewhere, but it was nowhere to be found. In the end Father Franciszek decided there was nothing else to do but trust in God's providence. The expected search was never carried out. Jokingly, but with relief, everyone agreed that they did not manage to plant the gun. On another occasion several expensive sheepskin coats belonging to the participants of the winter Oasis disappeared overnight. It was widely believed that the coats were removed by the Police in the hope that this would create an atmosphere of mistrust. Instead a special collection was taken up to replace the coats with everyone contributing.

Every participant in an Oasis retreat needs his own special notebook; there are also several textbooks used by both participants and Oasis leaders. These were printed in their thousands, in early Spring, without of course the authorities' consent. In time the Police managed to track down all cars used by the movement and they were frequently stopped by the traffic police for a "routine check". The driver and all passengers were usually detained for 48 hours and an "investigation" would begin. When they were released from their cells, all printed material confiscated from them remained in police custody. After a while an official letter would arrive informing them that the case against them had been dropped. The confiscated books and leaflets were never returned. After a few years, such losses were costing the Light–Life movement millions of złoty.

Some intimidations were aimed directly at Father Franciszek. In the severe winter of 1977 he was forbidden to buy any coal for the house in Krościenko where coal was the only means of heating. The news spread along the grapevine throughout Poland and in a few days thousands of small parcels each around a kilo in weight, began to arrive at Krościenko post office addressed to Father Blachnicki. Each contained a piece of coal; some also included fruit, a pair of gloves or a scarf. At the time a winter course for Oasis leaders was taking place in Krościenko. Every day at three o'clock all of them gathered outside the house and marched off to collect the parcels from the overflowing post office. To appease the post-office clerks most of the "goodies" sent with the coal were left at the post office as a token of appreciation for their additional work. Soon the authorities gave up and Father Franciszek was able to buy coal after all.

The main efforts of the authorities however, were directed towards hampering Oasis retreats. From the beginning Oasis had developed despite intimidation and pressure from the local state administration. Not a single retreat went by without some sort of government commission trying to "inspect" it. Over the years the "inspections" began to be looked on as a permanent feature so that on the occasions when it did not occur, everybody thought something was missing. It even became a joke to refer to the inspections as "visits" when two people came, and as a "raid" when there were several visitors. Whether it was a visit or a raid, the officials always tried to intimidate those in charge of the retreat and to obtain a list of all participants. Every inspection inevitably ended with a request for the immediate termination of the camp usually on the grounds of inadequate sanitation.

Administrative pressure, aimed at both the participants and the peasants giving them lodging, increased steadily, reaching its height in the summer of 1977. That year, Lech Bafia, the head of the local government in the Nowy Sącz region, where two thirds of Oasis retreats took place and where the national centre in Krościenko was situated, thought out a "final solution of the Oasis problem". He issued a decree on the "liquidation of all illegal youth camps in the region of Nowy Sącz". At the same time a confidential memo was sent out to all headmasters and local police stations explaining that the decree applied only to Oasis retreats. The headmasters and the Police were asked to locate Oasis centres and promptly report them to specially formed anti-Oasis squads – each consisting of a dozen or so people. They included representatives of various state authorities – the fire brigade, the local tax office, the security forces, the local education and sanitation departments. The whole operation was coordinated and supervised by a central unit in Nowy Sącz. All the squads started to operate at the beginning of the summer. Little did they know that the Oasis movement was well prepared for this offensive. For no sooner had Bafia issued his decree than it was photocopied by some friends of the Oasis Movement and passed on to Father Franciszek. By the time the first series of retreats began, a plan of defence had been discussed with all Oasis leaders. So when they were given orders to close down an "illegal camp" they argued: "You have come to the wrong place. We are not a youth camp but a retreat carried out on the instructions of the local bishop". The answer was that despite all this the inspection must still take place. It was not opposed but the officials were totally ignored and refused any cooperation or request to sign a protocol. Next day the retreat leader would receive an official order to close the "illegal youth camp" within 24 hours under threat of legal action. That year some 70 such orders were issued. In this situation the leaders never appealed to the higher authorities in the Communist system: "this means appealing from Lucifer to Beelzebub" as Father Blachnicki saw it. Instead the Oasis participants saw it as an opportunity to testify to their faith. A standard protest letter was sent back stating that Oasis retreats were based on God's law, international law and the Polish Constitution and were therefore legal, while the order demanding dissolution of the retreat was itself illegal and an act of religious persecution. "As the retreat is carried out on the instructions of the bishop we shall continue it," all the reply letters stated. "If you attempt to break up the retreat by force we will put up no resistance but will accept all the consequences, including intimidation and persecution, calmly and joyfully. Does the Bible not say 'Happy are those who are persecuted in the cause of right: theirs is the Kingdom of Heaven' (Matt. 5: 10). We also promise to include you in our prayers." Usually the matter came to an end at that point; it was clear that the authorities did not want to create martyrs. Instead their tactics changed. Intimidation was concentrated on the peasants giving lodgings to Oasis participants. They were threatened with heavy fines and in many cases fines were actually imposed. Of course, they were never fined directly for taking in young people from Oasis but rather for "not reporting lodgers to the police", "letting accommodation below the acceptable standard" or "not paying tax on additional income". Many peasants received the demand for payment of the fine on the eve of Pope John Paul II's first visit to Poland in June 1979.

The Polish Episcopate reacted sharply to the intimidation of Oasis retreats. A memorandum concerning the restrictions was sent to the Minister for Religious Affairs stating "The 'Oases' organised by the office for Liturgical Renewal take the form of retreats for young people. They aim to prepare participants for more meaningful religious experience. This Church ministry is in line with conciliar renewal. The retreats carried out by Oasis methods are organised under the auspices of the Conference of the Polish Episcopate. They are organised and personally led by priests acting on the basis of a decree issued by a bishop. Retreat activities take place in churches, chapels and other church premises. Participants rent private rooms in the same way as tourists. They prepare their own meals in kitchens and private homes. Therefore regulations concerning state-sponsored youth camps do not apply to them." As a supplement to the memorandum, the Plenary Conference of Bishops expressed the conviction that the Ministry of Liturgical Renewal should not encounter any sort of obstruction by the local authorities. The owners of buildings who make lodgings available to retreat participants should not be subject to harassment or sanctions. "Any activity of this kind, intended to impede such forms of ministry, must be regarded as a violation of constitutionally guaranteed religious freedom."

During this difficult time, Cardinal Wojtyła proved to be the staunchest defender of the Oasis Movement. He issued a special communiqué which was to be read out in all parish churches where Oasis retreats took place. It read, "Among many whom you took into your homes this Summer there are young people under the care of priests, nuns or lay Catholic activists. Those young people came to our parishes in order to attend summer holiday retreats – the so-called 'Oases'. Thank you very much for opening your homes to these young people, who want to live in the Spirit of the Gospel as true children of God. I have been informed that in some places the local authorities have tried to put pressure on the people offering lodgings to our Catholic youth. Owners of houses have been summoned for interrogations, policemen came round together with local bureaucrats and delivered them orders to rid themselves immediately of participants in an 'illegal youth camp'. If they refuse they are fined for a breach of the law. I wish to state publicly that the above mentioned forms of intimidation are illegal, represent the misuse of power by the local authorities and can only be described as religious discrimination. Oases are legal pastoral activities which have been carried on by the Church for several years and the government has never expressed any reservation about their existence. As the Oasis movement educates young people to become honest citizens serving God and their fellow man, and to accept high moral standards, they should in fact receive all possible support from the local authorities. We have the right to expect that our young people, like all other citizens, should be treated justly. We have the right to expect that no special decrees be issued concerning people offering lodgings to Oasis . . . I give my blessing to all those who open their hearts and homes for our Catholic youth this Summer, in a spirit of Christian hospitality and to those who freely accept persecution in the cause of righteousness."

That August, as usual, the Cardinal participated in the "community day", to manifest his support for Oasis. It was at this time that the future Pope John Paul II spoke forcibly of the Light-Life movement as the "frontline of the battle for man" in Poland. The highland people did not allow themselves to be intimidated and simply ignored all orders to evict "illegal tenants". However by the end of the summer all those who had let their houses or barns to Oasis received heavy fines or had extra taxes to pay. The Cardinal responded by writing letters to all those fined offering words of praise and consolation but also assuring them of financial help. Few people knew that it was in fact Cardinal Wojtyła who gave the money to pay all the fines that summer – some 70,000 złoty in all.

In 1978 even darker clouds began to gather over Oasis. A new tactic was adopted by the authorities – to persuade the Polish Episcopate that the Movement was interested only in anti-state and anti-socialist activities, pursuing political rather than spiritual goals. At the beginning of May, the Minister for Religious Affairs sent a letter to the Secretary of the Polish Episcopate sharply attacking the Light-Life movement. It was described as "illegal and infiltrated by political dissidents". In August another letter was sent, by Bafia this time, to Cardinal Wojtyła with a long list of accusations concerning the Light-Life movement and pointing out that Oasis retreats took place contrary to the law and binding decrees and also contrary to the model of a religious cult considered tolerable by the Polish communist authorities. The Cardinal replied at the end of September defending the Light-Life movement and its retreats. As in the summer of 1977, he issued a communiqué which was later read out in the parishes where Oasis retreats were held. In it the Cardinal once again warmly recommended the retreat groups to the priests and the whole parish community, and thanked all home owners who made lodgings available to the young Oasis participants.

However the intimidation of Oasis continued, especially the attempts to close down the retreats. At the end of the first series of retreats Bishop Błaszkiewicz, formerly in charge of the Movement, brought the matter into the open in a powerful sermon preached on the "community day". Praising the quest for God by young Polish people, the bishop said bitterly, "Many Oases leaders have been placed in a very difficult situation in the last two weeks. They were handed an order to dissolve illegal youth camps within 24 hours despite the fact that Oases are not camps but retreats. Are the Oases participants invaders or criminals? Are they people who have done wrong? These are Polish children, in defence of whom Father Blachnicki fought in 1939, in defence of whom I fought too . . . and I think we have a right now to go on defending the rights of men, children, Poles.

130

If a local authority official orders a priest to break up a retreat, he violates that priest's conscience. Article 82 of the Polish Constitution states: The Polish People's Republic guarantees freedom of conscience and creed for every citizen. A local bureaucrat who issues the order to break up a retreat is surely violating the Polish Constitution and in a lawful state he would have been brought before a court for violating freedom of conscience. In addition, the Polish Constitution states that, 'no one may forcibly prevent a citizen from participating in a religious ceremony.' Many of you are over eighteen, so you are full citizens. If a local bureaucrat orders you to leave the retreat this violates the Constitution for the second time. Woe betide a state which issues decrees and passes a constitution and then shamelessly and publicly breaks them. It is even more scandalous that the violation takes place in front of young people, who have been taught about the Constitution at school. On 12 December 1966 Poland signed a pact on human and civil rights at the United Nations. It was ratified by the Polish People's Republic on 3 March 1977. I would like to quote article 18 point 4 of this pact: 'the countries which are signatories of this pact are bound to respect the right of the family to religious education of the children in accordance with conviction.' As all of you who are not yet eighteen had brought a letter from your parents agreeing to your participation in Oasis, the order to dissolve the Oasis retreat violates this pact also. In the name of our Constitution, of man's freedom and also of legality, we must protest most strongly against this evident religious discrimination. Is it not sad that a bishop has to defend law and order in the country? I have told you all this so you would know the truth and not to arouse your indignation or, God forbid, your hatred. We are capable of suffering, but also of forgiveness. We can and do love our enemies. However this does not exclude our right and indeed our duty to defend the rights of man."

Again, as in previous years, not one Oasis dissolved itself. Nevertheless there remained the problem of heavy fines imposed on peasants. Father Blachnicki did not dare to ask Cardinal Wojtyła again for help. Instead, each retreat leader was made responsible for finding enough people to pay part of the fine so that the whole sum could be divided into token amounts of ten zloty – at that time something like ten pence. Then everyone sent their ten zloty to the regional magistrate in the name of the homeowner. Soon local authorities all over the south of Poland were flooded by hundreds of ten zloty postal orders, while the forms for purchasing postal orders became scarce indeed. For a time the authorities gave in and the fines stopped.

On 16 October 1978 Cardinal Wojtyła became Pope John Paul II and the Light-Life movement lost its greatest supporter and defender. The tactics used against the movement were changed again. With Pope John Paul II far away in Rome, the state authorities decided on a policy intended to discredit the Movement in the eyes of the Polish Episcopate and to cut it off from John Paul II. Anonymous memoranda and appeals alleging "serious doctrinal deviations" within the movement were circulated among the Polish hierarchy and clergy. People posing as Oasis members openly criticised the bishops and traditional methods of pastoral work, "popular religiosity" in particular. False statements and letters, probably written by the secret police but "signed" by Father Blachnicki, were widely disseminated in Poland. Some of Father Blachnicki's original letters were "improved" and then circulated among bishops and clergy. In one letter some twenty vital changes were made. For example the sentence, "One must follow one's conscience and not obey the authorities blindly" had "even the Church authorities" added to it. "Our Polish bishops" was changed into "our backward Polish bishops" etc. Letters, mostly anonymous, began to arrive at various diocesan curias, demanding immediate action against Father Blachnicki. The authorities' aim was clear. They hoped to kill the Light-Life movement through action taken by the Polish bishops. The longstanding supporters of the movement, such as Bishop J. Tokarczuk of Przemyśl and Bishop T. Błaszkiewicz of Tarnów, had no doubt that most of the problems with Light-Life were the doing of the authorities, but some bishops unfortunately seemed to be unsure of Light-Life. At one stage the continuation of Oasis retreats was discussed by the entire Episcopate at its plenary conference. It seemed quite possible that the bishops would forbid the continuation of the Oases. Father Blachnicki ordered preparations for the summer programme to go ahead but everybody knew that he would never go against a decision by the bishops. Would the authorities succeed at last? What was to become of the movement? The Crusade? The atmosphere at the house in Krościenko was tense; the strain was only too visible on Father Franciszek's face. On the day of the bishops' conference Father Franciszek came down to breakfast cheerful. "I think we are saved," he announced to his astounded associates. "I had a dream last night that I was sentenced to death. I was ordered to go and check whether my name was on the execution list. I went to the table and loudly pronounced my name: Blachnicki. A gloomy person looked up and down the list again and again. Then he lifted his head and told me, "You are not on the list, go home." By the end of the day the bishops' decision had reached Krościenko. The Oases were to be continued.

Probably hoping for an altogether different decision the local authorities had not prepared themselves properly and the intimidation of the retreats lessened visibly. Nevertheless several incidents did occur – among them confiscation of 4000 copies of the Gospel of St Luke which were to be used in the Crusade. The Bibles were found in an Oasis car by militiamen and confiscated on the spot as "illegal publications". A criminal charge was brought against the driver of the car. A strongly worded memorandum, signed by Father Blachnicki and other leaders of the Light-Life movement, was sent to Cardinal Wyszyński, the head of the Polish Roman Catholic Church.

"The Bible is seen by all people, regardless of their creed, as having a unique value, one which influenced the formation of Christian culture, which promoted respect for man and his dignity. Therefore treating the Bible as an 'illegal' or 'criminal' publication can only be seen as an unprecedented manifestation of barbarism." Referring to the Soviet Union the memorandum stated, "We know that for some years some of our neighbouring states have been treating the Bible at Customs in the same way as pornographic literature and imprisoning people for its distribution. These facts should be branded as a disgrace to twentieth-century civilisation. We still remember the moving appeal of

John Paul II in defence of human rights, which he gave in the grounds of the wartime Nazi concentration camp of Brzezinka where four million people were killed. When the Bible, which reveals the full extent of human dignity, is treated as illegal and criminal material, is this not the first step towards the creation of a mentality which finally leads to horrifying crimes against humanity? We appeal to the Conference of Bishops to lodge the strongest possible protest with the Polish authorities as well as with international human-rights institutions, against this attempt to transfer to Poland methods which until now have been used by the atheist authorities in neighbouring states."

It was also in the summer of 1979 that an unexplained fire broke out in a newly-built house where participants in the Oasis retreat were staying. The fire mysteriously started in a farm building where sheep were kept and where there was no chimney, no stove, not even an electrical installation. The police investigating team promptly arrived from Nowy Sącz. Perhaps not too surprisingly they were recognised as belonging to anti-Oasis squads. It soon became evident that they had come in the conviction that the fire was started by Oasis people and were determined to prove this. To some people being interviewed Oasis guilt was gently suggested. A militiaman tried to persuade a witness to state under oath that there was a door between the farm building and the part where participants of Oasis slept, even though there was never such a door. Indignation was also caused by the conduct of the militiamen towards the owner of the house. Whilst still in an immediate state of shock and suffering from serious burns, he was exposed to two hours of unpleasant interrogation – not about the fire but about his Oasis lodgers. The interrogation was stopped only after a group leader came in and took the peasant out of the room. By then his condition had deteriorated so much that he had to be taken to hospital. The next day a collection was organised among all participants in the retreats and given to the unfortunate man.

Hardly a week had passed since the tragic night of the fire when a local paper *Gazeta Południowa* gave a very different picture of events. In an article entitled, "On the safety of children at Summer camps", it alleged that an illegal youth camp organised by irresponsible adults who did not care much for the safety of children, was established in a primitive, high fire-risk house. "It was a miracle that nobody was killed," the article went on, "hopefully this will serve as a warning to all those who endanger the lives of children. If not a law will have to be passed to prevent any similar or even greater tragedy." This ominous article alarmed the leaders of the Light-Life movement. Were the authorities ready to risk the lives of children in a better organised fire in order to push through the law on "illegal camps"?

Since its 1980 declaration, the Light-Life movement has become a special object of interest to the Ministry of Religious Affairs. Special memoranda were sent to the Polish hierarchy accusing the movement of taking part in political activities and allying itself with the political opposition. The smear campaign against Father Blachnicki continued with the appearance of letters allegedly written by him. Many found their way to Krościenko. Father Franciszek decided to photocopy the discrediting letters and send them to the Pope – just to inform him of what was happening. Soon after

Cardinal Wyszyński received an official Decretus Laudis from the Roman Curia with an order to read it to Bishop Błaszkiewicz – who was in charge of Oasis.

"Through correspondence and conversations I am struck by the great Christian maturity with which you are handling various matters, particularly the difficult ones, in your personal as well as in your communal life. Yes, only in faith does a person find the truth, the full truth about that which is within himself and around him. The times in which we live demand such faith from Christians today – simple, child-like faith, but at the same time conscious, mature and tested. Therefore I am glad that you are directing your young hearts and thoughts in precisely this direction. It is there that you are seeking and finding the truth about yourselves and others. I rejoice and thank God that the young people of Poland, as well as the youth of various countries around the world, are turning in this direction. I observe this with great hope, an open heart, and tremendous thankfulness to Christ the Lord and His Immaculate Mother. Through the disappointments and painful experiences which past generations have endured and which the present generation unfortunately continues to experience, God is visiting His people in a special way. This is also a sign, a sign of our times, which we must interpret with great sensitivity and readiness of heart.

"So how can we not be thankful to God, seeing that you are endeavouring to live out the great and unrepeatable adventure of your youth in a special way, in spiritual communion with Christ. This way, the way of spiritual communion and openness toward one's neighbour, was ordained by God in the mystery of Creation. It was confirmed and perfected by Christ, who brought the Church into being as the community of God's people

"Upon you, Your Excellency, patron of the Light–Life movement, on the Church's behalf, and upon His Excellency the National Coordinator; upon the regional leaders and upon all Oases and their members, I bestow the Apostolic Blessing with my whole heart."

If the letter finally reconciled all bishops to the movement it also marked the beginning of a new wave of intimidation of Father Blachnicki and Oasis participants. The fining of peasant home-owners, who gave lodgings to Oasis participants, was resumed. American friends from the Agape movement who were visiting the retreats received notice to leave Poland. Members of the movement were refused passports to travel to Italy for the Roman Oasis. When Father Franciszek too was refused a passport to visit the West, he responded with an open letter written to the Polish Minister of Internal Affairs.

"Since the very inception of the present political system of the Polish People's Republic, the passport policy of the security police has been an instrument for the limitation of freedom, the discrimination, vexation and blackmail of citizens, and the violation and deprivation of conscience.

"In every state of the world with a democratic system the permanent possession of a passport is an expression of citizens' rights, viewed in the same way as the possession of a personal identity card. In Poland, on the other hand, receiving a passport is an act of grace on the part of the security police. No one knows what must be done to merit it, and when one does one feels as though one had been released from prison. In the company of people from free, democratic states, we must constantly appear as slaves, answering invitations to take part in various meetings with: 'I don't know whether I will receive a passport, or whether I will receive one in time, or whether they will let me go. That is to say nothing of the fact that even when we finally 'succeed' in travelling abroad, we must then appear to the world as beggars, unable to support ourselves with our own Polish money.

"It therefore seems high time that this humiliating and disgraceful situation be changed. The present situation provides constant proof to the world that values such as democracy, civil liberties and the rights and dignity of the individual are a myth in Poland.

"In formulating the above protest against the restrictions of individual rights and liberties on the basis of the passport law of 17 June 1959, I am speaking not only for myself but for about three hundred other people as well, throughout the entire country, who were refused passports by the security police in May and June of this year. These would have enabled them to travel to Rome to take part in a pilgrimage and a fifteen-day guided retreat by the so-called Oasis method. This group was made up primarily of high-school and university students who wanted to travel to Rome for purely religious reasons, at the invitation of Pope John Paul II. They were clearly aware that the refusal represented religious persecution and discrimination, all the more so since functionaries of the security police, in conversations with priests and young people, repeatedly and openly confirmed that the refusal to give them passports stemmed from the trip's purpose, participation in a so-called Oasis retreat, that is practising their religion. So in addition, what has taken place here is an open violation of article 18 of the Covenant on Civil and Political Rights cited above, which reads: 'Everyone has the right to freedom of thought, conscience and religion.' This right embraces the freedom to express one's convictions or practise one's religion whether as an individual or together with others, publicly or privately, by worship as well as training and instruction.

"I would also like to protest in the name of my closest associates, priests as well as lay-people, who in the past several years have systematically been refused passports because of their association with me.

"Since the situation described above, which results from the present passport law and the policies of the security police, amount to the restriction of freedom, and thus a form of imprisonment, you will find enclosed with this document my personal identity card (No. ZN 1988677), which I am relinquishing to the Ministry of Internal Affairs. After all, prisoners do not carry their personal identity documents with them, but must surrender them to the prison authorities. I do not desire to maintain the illusion, created by carrying a personal identity card, that I am a free person when in fact this freedom is denied me.

"I would also like to contribute in this way to the acceleration of the process of authentic democratisation and national liberation. Among other things, this process must include a change in the passport law, giving citizens permanent passports and the right to cross the border at any time, as long as there is no legitimate cause properly verified by due process of law, to restrict this freedom for the common good."

The authorities gave in and Father Franciszek was allowed to travel to the West.

8

One Freedom – in God

On 10 December 1981 Father Franciszek left Poland for an urgent meeting in Germany with Bishop Szcze-pan Wesoły, who was the bishop delegate for all Poles residing outside Poland. The trip was to be short, just ten days, so he could be back for Christmas at Krościenko. He did not know that he was never to see Krościenko again. Father Franciszek was to open a new chapter in the history of the Light-Life movement; his meeting with the bishop was to discuss the details of the movement's acquisition of a former orphanage in Carlsberg – a small village situated on the verge of a beautifully picturesque national park, Pfalzer Wald, in West Germany.

The orphanage, originally built by Polish émigrés and run by Polish nuns, had outlived its usefulness. At one stage there were 80 Polish children living there. Over the years however the number of children had steadily declined and since 1979 the centre had been standing virtually empty. Bishop Wesoły knew that for sometime Father Franciszek had been searching for a building to house an International Centre for the Light-Life movement. By the end of the 1970s the movement had begun to take root in such diverse countries as Bolivia and India. A centre outside Poland was essential so that national animators and moderators could be trained without interference from the Polish authorities, but also so that the movement's Christian formation of young people could be promoted among the Churches worldwide. A special team had already been undergoing intensive training in Poland to run the future International Centre. The orphanage in Carlsberg seemed to be God-sent. Father Franciszek arrived in Germany in September to discuss the possible takeover, however all plans were suddenly brought to a halt when someone stole his travelling bag in a coffee shop in Frankfurt railway station. In it were all the documents including his passport so Father Franciszek had to return and apply for a new one. Bureaucracy dragged out the processing of his application and Bishop Wesoły along with the trustees of the orphanage were getting impatient. Articles appeared in the regional papers pressing for the transfer of the abandoned orphanage to the German Caritas movement to save it from dilapidation. Urgent action was necessary yet Father Franciszek was stranded in Poland. "At the time," he later confessed, "I was annoyed a little with my guardian angel, for allowing the theft and complicating matters. Then I reflected and decided to trust in God's providence."

Finally the passport came through. Three days after leaving Poland, on Sunday 13 December, Father Franciszek was to celebrate Mass in a small German town. He was putting his vestments on when he was told that martial law had been imposed in Poland. At first the country was so securely cut-off from the rest of the world that it took a few weeks before Father Franciszek could assess the impact of martial law on the Light-Life movement. Many members who were actively involved in Solidarity were arrested or interned; many lost their jobs. However, none of the movement centres were searched and the permanent diaconate also remained untouched. As all gatherings had been declared illegal, apart from assemblies in church for religious services, the Movement limited its activities to prayer and charitable work within the parishes. Father Franciszek looked back at the incident with the passport in September and reflected "was it just an incident or a sign of God's providence." If he had returned to Poland then he would most probably have been interned sooner rather than later. From the West, he could help the Light-Life movement and his country to the best of his abilities, unhindered. After obtaining consent from Cardinal Józef Glemp – the Primate of Poland – Father Franciszek settled in Carlsberg. Within a few months a small community of some twenty people was already working full time to renovate the whole centre. Living in a spirit of comradeship, like the first Christians, all members of the group joined in a special continuous programme of spiritual development prepared by Father Franciszek – The International Light-Life Centre for Evangelisation had become a fact.

The centre progressed quickly towards becoming a Krościenko in the West – émigré Poles soon learnt about "Marianum", as the centre was called, and began to descend on Carlsberg, especially during religious feastdays. Already in the summer of 1982, 250 people participated in the first Carlsberg-based Oasis retreats. Since then Oasis retreats have become a permanently recurring feature of the Carlsberg calendar. Several groups, mainly Polish, have also been following post-Oasis programmes, not only in Germany but also in other European countries. Evangelical retreats using the film "Jesus" have been carried out in Polish parishes in Germany, England and Sweden, where it was the first retreat in Polish since 1945.

The Carlsberg yearly school for animators has been continuously busy training animators not only for Poland but also for Argentina, Paraguay and Bolivia, where the Light-Life movement, first introduced there by Polish missionaries in 1978, has developed rapidly. Since December 1982, within the centre, a publishing house called "Maximilianum" has been operating. The books are later distributed in Poland. It was also at Carlsberg – out of reach of the Polish security police – that Father Franciszek continued his work on the Polish theology of liberation. The introduction of martial law had only strengthened his conviction that the programme of liberation through truth was the only way which guaranteed success. The theme of liberation through truth became central to most of Father Franciszek's articles, meditations, lectures and addresses. Also, at his suggestion, a "Christian Service for the Liberation of Nations through Truth" (ChSWN) came into being at Carlsberg in June 1982 to extend moral and spiritual help to Poland, in its struggle for full liberation, as well as to all other countries enslaved by Soviet communism. Rejecting political goals and means, ChSWN was to concentrate on supporting and actively pursuing programmes of evangelisation among enslaved nations, promoting both individual and group prayers for the liberation of nations, distribution of Bibles and spiritual literature, and building unity and cooperation among all Christian movements, missions and organisations with similar aims. ChSWN proved to be a dynamic and fruitful association.

In August 1982 it came up with the so called "Carlsberg Declaration" containing a long term programme of action for the Liberation of Poland, deeply rooted in Father Blachnicki's theology of liberation. At its heart lies the concept of "internal sovereignty" which can be achieved through voluntary acceptance of God-given values, especially the value of truth and life regardless of consequences. "The sovereignty of an individual courageously bearing witness to the truth," stated the declaration, "is an important victory over the system of enslavement based on lies and fear. That is why educating people and leading them to achieve internal sovereignty, disseminating information about examples of courageous witness to the truth and making people realise its value, are of paramount importance in the spiritual struggle for liberation from Soviet totalitarianism. The highest level of sovereignty is achieved by a man who in his struggle for liberation rejects hatred and the use of force. Opposing force with force should be recognised as an out of date bygone formula for revolution. Contemporary humanity has worked out a new form of revolution, which excludes the use of violence and force, which raises the dignity of man and makes him truly sovereign. However this revolution requires a high moral integrity of its leaders. They have to realise that in following this path they achieve a higher level of internal sovereignty, regardless of whether they achieve external success in the process of struggle or become a victim."

The authors of the "Declaration" were well aware that to achieve internal sovereignty, a man needs a small community where he can find help and support. "The most obvious and smallest community where all members can best encourage each other on the way to internal sovereignty is of course a family. Alongside the family, national networks of other groups should be formed – educational, self-help and charitable groups." The Declaration argued that the more such groups existed the greater the sphere of freedom, within the whole of society, would be extended, bringing about liberation of entire social groups like peasants and workers, as well as the formation of a free and independent culture. The conclusion was that political sovereignty would be a natural and an almost unavoidable consequence.

In November 1982, at the initiative of ChSWN, forty-five delegates representing eight countries of the Soviet Bloc, came to Carlsberg to try to find a common way towards liberation. All unanimously accepted that the "Carlsberg Declaration", inspired by the Christian vision of man, had to become an essential part of the programme for the Liberation of Nations of Central and Eastern Europe – all strongly linked with Christianity through their history and culture.

Since then a number of similar symposia and congresses have been organised, as well as the annual "March for the Liberation of Nations" – all aimed at promoting the programme of liberation as well as building up solidarity among all Soviet-dominated nations. They also tried to place before the conscience of the world the fate of the European nations which have unwillingly become part of the Soviet Empire.

When in December 1981 Father Franciszek decided to remain in the West some were worried that without its charismatic leader and founder, the Light-Life movement would disintegrate. However, the vast majority saw Father Blachnicki's absence as a challenge to continue his spiritual mission as well as a verification of the movement's Christian maturity and the spiritual maturity of every individual member. Father Franciszek retained the title of national moderator but it was obvious that someone would have to run the movement from inside Poland. The Polish Episcopate delegated Father Wojciech Danielski, one of Father Franciszek's closest associates, to carry on this difficult task. Father Danielski proved to be the right person at the right time. A gentle man, he attached great importance to details, analysing every matter with almost microscopic accuracy. These qualities helped him to consolidate all the diverse programmes and activities pursued within the movement. On the initiative of Father Danielski a national council of moderators consisting of ten priests was created. It was now the council rather than a national moderator which assumed responsibility for the spiritual aspect of the entire movement. A mixed council, consisting of priests and lay people, was also created to try and legalise the ownership of some eighteen houses left to the movement by its friends and sympathisers. For years Father Danielski had been an administrator of a boarding house for priests studying at the Catholic University of Lublin. It was there that he had formed close friendships with many students and future bishops. As a leader of the movement he embarked on a trip almost in the style of St Paul.

He visited all of Poland's dioceses and relying on his friendships, managed to awaken in many bishops a deep sense of responsibility for the movement within their dioceses. Indeed since 1981 every diocese has had a dedicated diocesan moderator appointed by the local bishop in cooperation with Krościenko.

The bishops' increasingly direct involvement in the movement soon became clear. Rarely did a community day at Oasis pass without a local bishop joining in. Moreover the organisation of summer retreats, post-Oasis development and retreats for animators and moderators, the promotion of the Crusade for the Liberation of Man, the distribution of printed aids – all tasks once pursued almost solely by the centre in Krościenko – became the responsibility of each diocese and of the local bishop.

For years the Light-Life movement was forced to produce its ever-increasing printed materials illegally, using primitive duplicators, hidden in remote villages. Father Danielski was determined to change this state of affairs. He pleaded so long with Cardinal Franciszek Macharski of Kraków that the latter agreed not only to publish the movement's printed aids in the diocesan publishing house but he also gave the Church imprimatur to all materials used for the spiritual development programme.

Thanks to Father Danielski's perseverance, a pastoral and liturgical course for priests was created at the Catholic University of Lublin in October 1984. Six times a year diocesan and monastic priests, who act as moderators all over the country, arrive there to attend a three day programme of intensive lectures and spiritual exercises. This course plays an important part in Father Danielski's plans to develop the movement in depth rather than horizontally in members. Among all his various endeavours and aims, one was particularly crucial to him – to instil in every member of the vast Light-Life community a desire to strive for perfection and to share this way of life with others. By the time of Father Danielski's death on Christmas Eve 1985, there were over 70,000 people, mostly young, participating annually in the summer Oasis retreats and continuing their post-Oasis development throughout the year. There were also over 8,000 family circles scattered all over Poland and the membership of the Crusade for the Liberation of Man had increased to 50,000; all pledging total alcohol abstinence.

After the funeral on 30 December all the movement's moderators met to appoint a new leader. Father Henryk Bolczyk, a parish priest from Katowice, in the south of Poland, was chosen. Significantly he decided not to relinquish his former duties but to combine his parish ministry with the leadership of the Light-Life movement. His decision almost symbolically accentuated the ultimate aim of the movement: the renewal of every individual parish.

The 1980s have been marked by an all out campaign against the movement in the state-owned mass media. During the last few years countless anti-Light-Life articles have been published in both local and national papers. Few were concerned with analysing the movement, its origins, aims, methods or finances. Most were personal attacks on Father Blachnicki. Typical of this kind was a series of articles by Mr Sylwester Wlodarczyk which appeared in *Sztandar Młodych* at the beginning of 1983. The readers were "informed" that Father Blachnicki had entered a seminary in 1945 with only one aim in mind – "to create an independent, anti-socialist political movement". Hence Oasis retreats were nothing but a method used by him to indoctrinate young vulnerable people into the belief that "all evil in the world stems from Communism, which is why it must be fought mercilessly". In 1950, Mr Włodarczyk "revealed", Father Blachnicki had organised a Crusade "against socialism and all progressive social movements" behind the veil of an anti-alcohol campaign. The authorities had no choice but to arrest him. Later, after his release, Father Blachnicki began creating a so-called "new church". In time, continued Włodarczyk, Father Blachnicki decided that the Oases themselves were not enough and a "Christian Service" for Liberation was set up whose programme called for a merciless struggle against the state and for Poland to leave the Soviet Bloc. Since 1981, he had been running an extensive propaganda campaign from his base, mobilising western people against Poland. His ideas had gained many sympathisers in circles hostile to Poland. Thanks to them, Father Blachnicki could establish a centre at Carlsberg. Mr Wlodarczyk himself confessed that his research findings could easily be dismissed as tendentious if his picture of Oasis was not backed up by highly critical opinions expressed by the inhabitants of Krościenko – all of whom were met by chance by Mr Włodarczyk and needless to say were "devout Catholics". Conveniently enough all the critics, with the exception of a member of an anti-Oasis squad, asked to remain anonymous. Equally anonymous were letters to *Sztandar Młodych* supporting Mr Włodarczyk's analysis of the movement on the basis of their own "personal experience".

The articles on Father Blachnicki proved beyond doubt that it was his Theology of Liberation and his activity at Carlsberg which were at the core of the anti-Light-Life campaign. Poles were told again and again that the person whom they thought to be the leader of a religious movement of spiritual renewal was in fact a theologian of hatred, of counter-revolution and even of national treason; he was called a "Polish Ayatollah", a fanatical politician and a beloved child of Radio Free Europe.

This witch-hunt against Father Blachnicki and the Light-Life movement was also an indication of how worried the Party was about Father Blachnicki's concept of Liberation taking deep roots in Poland. Indeed the Polish mass media were joined by the Soviet press in their attacks. Then in the summer of 1983, Keston College, a research centre based in Kent, studying religion under communism, received a copy of *Notebook of Political documentation No. 4*, published for internal use by the information department of the Polish Party's Central Committee. The Notebook, dated March 1983, of which 21,000 copies were printed, contained significant documentation about the Christian Service for the Liberation of Nations (ChSWN). In a four-page note by some party ideologists, ChSWN is described as "an active centre for anti-communist revolution" and "politically extremist", expressing as its admitted aim "the ideological struggle for souls". ChSWN is seen by the party as an extension of the Light-Life movement and an attempt to apply its Liberation Theology to other countries of Eastern Europe. In addition to the notes, the party booklet reprinted all of the most important ChSWN documents. Ironically until then most members of the Light-Life movement knew the works Father Blachnicki had written outside Poland, as well as the text of the Carlsberg Declaration, only from slanderous articles in the press. Now they became available thanks to the Party's information department and a well wisher who had passed on a copy of the Notes to the movement.

For a long time there was no response from the Polish Episcopate; it usually prefers to deal with problems in a confidential manner outside the journalistic limelight. However, in a collection of interviews with famous Poles, published in Warsaw in 1985, Jan Dobraczyński, a well-known Polish Catholic writer (but totally subservient to the Polish authorities) accused Father Blachnicki of defaming Cardinal Wyszyński, collaborating with Communists and thus hastening his death. This time the authorities had overstepped the line. Bishop Blaszkiewicz responded with a strong statement condemning Dobraczyński's accusation as an outright lie. The text of the statement was to be published by the only national Catholic weekly *Tygodnik Powszechny* but it was confiscated by the censors.

All slanderous articles finding their way to Carlsberg were read carefully and filed away. Father Franciszek was well aware that some people inside Poland feared fresh repressions against the movement unless Father Franciszek abandoned his "political activity which was arousing the fury of the authorities". Was it not reasonable to expect Father Franciszek to think first and foremost about the future of the movement? In February 1983, in a letter addressed to the movement's leaders gathered at an annual congress at the monastery of Jasna Góra in Częstochowa, Father Franciszek had given a straightforward answer to this question.

"The Light-Life movement is a Polish phenomenon on such a scale that the attitude of the Polish authorities to it does not depend only on the activity of one individual, unless this is used as a pretext for an attack. The Light-Life movement shows the workings of the Holy Spirit at a given point in history. That is why it cannot refrain from doing what its conscience tells it, what its conscience compels it to do because of certain human fears. I should like to remind you that there has always been a specific logic of faith in the history of our movement and only thanks to this has our movement grown – contrary to all human considerations and human logic. The Light-Life movement would not exist now if we had made its growth dependent on opportunities granted to us by an atheist, totalitarian state. The movement is the fruit of supernatural courage linked with faith. The courage to follow only God's call and the call of one's conscience. It is in this spirit – free from fear, and trusting in God – that the movement should take upon itself the mission of educating a 'New Man', a man who lives out his faith and becomes a sign of hope to his brothers."

Soviet totalitarianism is the radical antithesis of the idea of human freedom. It is but a carefully thought out system of enslaving men and entire nations on a global scale. In this system a man can be only an object which is manipulated, which serves to strengthen the system's power. The system aims at destroying in man all that determines human dignity and freedom. However, it is in this system that a peaceful liberation movement has developed based on a vision of human freedom fulfilling itself by serving truth through love – creating a liberated "Man of the East".

This vision appears today in the resolve not only of individuals but of whole movements like Solidarity and the dissident movements in the Soviet Union. It is man who preserves his dignity and freedom even in prison or in an internment camp, man who perseveres on the road to liberty and self-respect despite intimidation and persecution. Obviously many people in Eastern Europe, maybe even the majority, still remain enslaved by fear. However, it cannot be denied that at no other time in the history of mankind have there been so many free people ready to make sacrifices for the sake of their freedom and dignity, as in Poland and other countries enslaved by Soviet communism.

The existence of this example of a "free man" is a basis for hope for the full liberation of these nations in the future. At the root of this hope there are countless martyrs, who paid the highest price for their devotion to spiritual freedom.

What about the "free" West however? It is common knowledge that dissidents thrown out of the Soviet Union suffer disappointment after encountering the free West. They are disappointed especially when in discussions they discover that in the name of pluralism, the ideas of absolute values and truth have virtually disappeared; that people are not even interested in discovering where the truth lies so that all could accept it. Someone once said – "If in the East a man says two time two equals five, we respond – you are a fool. In the West the response would be 'everybody is entitled to their opinion.'"

The Western notion of freedom develops not in confrontation with a totalitarian system but alongside a hedonistic and consumer system of civilisation. Freedom is understood as the possibility of options – a choice among many is possible. Of course the choice is usually subjective – I choose this because I like it, because it is nice, because it is profitable for me. Freedom becomes self-will. Hence, the chaos and powerlessness in solving serious problems that often face Western democracies, as well as the virtual collapse of moral values among young generations in the West.

The problem of the Liberation of Man and of whole societies is thus also significant for the free West – here the experiences of people from the East can be of enormous help in solving Western problems. In the end man will always remain the central problem and the lack of a true vision of man, the lack of understanding of human freedom, is in the final analysis the source of social, economic, political and cultural crisis.

The future holds more fear for the fate of Western civilisation than for that of nations of Eastern Europe. History teaches us that nations somehow solve the problem of enslavement by tyrants – but many nations have disappeared because of their own decadence.